Thos Griffith

THE STATE HOUSE AT ANNAPOLIS.

SKETCHES OF THE EARLY HISTORY OF MARYLAND

Thomas W. Griffith

HERITAGE BOOKS
2025

HERITAGE BOOKS

AN IMPRINT OF HERITAGE BOOKS, INC.

Books, CDs, and more—Worldwide

For our listing of thousands of titles see our website
at
www.HeritageBooks.com

A Facsimile Reprint
Published 2025 by
HERITAGE BOOKS, INC.
Publishing Division
5810 Ruatan Street
Berwyn Heights, MD 20740

Originally published
BALTIMORE:
Printed and Published by Frederick G. Schaeffer.
1824

— Publisher's Notice —
In reprints such as this, it is often not possible to remove blemishes from the original. We feel the contents of this book warrant its reissue despite these blemishes and hope you will agree and read it with pleasure.

International Standard Book Number
Paperbound: 978-0-7884-4814-0

SKETCHES

OF THE

EARLY HISTORY

OF

MARYLAND.

IN the year 1634, Leonard Calvert, appointed Lieutenant-general and Governor of Maryland, by his brother Cecelius, Lord Baltimore and proprietary, George Calvert, another brother, and about two hundred colonists, having sailed from England the year before, and wintered in the West India islands, landed and fixed themselves on the north side of the Patowmack river, a few miles from the mouth of it, and called the place St. Mary's.

This was effected without any opposition from the natives of the country, who it would appear according to Mr. Bozman's researches, were subjects of Opitchapan, Powhatan's successor or of the same confederacy, and governed by a youthful Werowance or viceroy and a regent of the name of Archihan. They received a satisfactory compensation, were much reduced and terrified by their northern neighbours of red men, and willing to receive the protection of allies so enlightened and warlike as were the new colonists.

These being in part, gentlemen of affluence, well provided, arriving at a favorable season, and countenanced, though not encouraged, and sometimes opposed by the earlier settlements of the Virginia colonists on the south, and the Swedes and Dutch on the north, did not encounter the distress and defeats which had usually attended such settlements. Besides the Governor and his brother, we find the names of Jerome Hawley, Thomas Cornwallis, Richard Gerrard, Edward Wintour, Frederick Wintour and Henry Wiseman, Esqs. Capt. John Hill and Messrs. John Saunders, Edward Cranfield, Henry Green, Nicholas Fairfax, John Baxter, Thomas Derrel, John Medcalfe, and William Saire, of whom, Messrs. Hawley and Cornwallis were appointed by Lord Baltimore, to be assistants to the Governor, or Councillors. Captain Henry Fleete, who they found at Piscataway on landing, assisted them materially.

They lived in the same houses, and cultivated the same grounds with the red people, and in the utmost harmony, until one of the Virginia council, named William Clayborne, who had procured a license to trade, and established factories on Kent Island and near the Susquehannah, excited the Indians living within the territories granted to Lord Baltimore, but who were pacified or overawed when the Governor had forcibly dispersed the intruders soon after.

George Calvert, the first Baron of Baltimore and father of the proprietary, who had named the son after his patron, Robert Cecil, Earl of Salsbury, was born at Kipling in Yorkshire and educated at Oxford University, which he represented in Parliament afterwards; filling the office of Secretary of State, but was rather one of the Secretaries of the Council of State as then organized, and the King had granted him part of Newfoundland, which he called Avalon, visited and made some improvements there, but vainly attempted to colonize. He had been one of the society or company for settling Virginia in 1620, and had, on account of difficulties encountered during his residence there, as a Roman Catholic, to which religion he had become a convert and thereby forfeited all his offices, except that of a Privy Councillor, in which he was continued during the life of James I. the promise of another particular grant from the King; it was rather an exemption from the forfeiture incurred by that company, than an encroachment on former grants, for the successor to the crown to bestow on Cecilius the son, the unsettled lands on the Chesapeake, and from the sea to the source of the Patowmack; the former were supposed to extend from the 38th to the 40th degree of north latitude, as described in the charter, and Sir John Harvey, the then viceroy of Virginia, politely waited on and tendered his civilities to his brother, the Governor.

In that act, the province which Lord Baltimore intended to call Crescentia, was named Maryland, by King Charles, in honor of his royal consort, who was Henrietta-Maria, daughter of Henry IV. of France.

It does not appear that these colonists were actuated by an over pious zeal to convert the heathen, or the extravagant project of finding a passage to the east through the western continent; but, out of respect for their religion, they planted the cross, and after fortifying themselves, plainly and openly set about to obtain by the fairest means in their power, other property and homes, where they should escape the persecutions of the religious and political reformers of their native country at that period.

The land was granted Lord Baltimore according to the most liberal *tenure* of the times, two Indian arrows a year; the colonists were exempted from English customs or taxes here, and entitled to protection from that kingdom, at home or abroad, as native born subjects. Although there were clauses which a British attorney-general in 1680, declared to be, "not agreeable to the laws there," laws could only be made here with the advice and consent of the freemen or their deputies; and, if amongst the grants, there was power to make ordinances given to the proprietaries, there is an exception of much liberality towards the people, which was, that, "no person should be deprived of member, life, freehold, goods or chattles," by such ordinances; and the act became a model for succeeding grants.

According to the conditions of plantation of the proprietary, as contained in "*The Landholder's Assistant*," each colonist was entitled to *one hundred acres* for himself, as much for his wife and *fifty acres* a piece for his children and servants, in perpetuity, on payment of *twenty pounds of wheat* per hundred acres, per annum. There were to be baronies as well as manors for larger tracts, than which there could not be a greater inducement for independent settlers; and some, by paying the passages of others, obtained, with their services, the land rights of upwards of twenty persons or two thousand and three thousand acres ; no privileges were enjoyed for such large estates except that of being able to lease them out again, and no baronies were ever granted, though a court-baron and court-leet were held on one or two occasions, and there was a fine or tax, upon sales of land, equal to the quit rent of a year, on each sale or alienation ; for a majority of the *freeholders* here, would necessarily be composed of lesser tenants, and feudal service was becoming odious every where.

With expressions of gratitude for his personal exertions, the proprietary added to his brother's powers, those of Admiral, Chief Judge and Chancellor ; and it is stated that the Governor immediately proceeded to appoint a Secretary and Sheriff, military officers, Commissioners of the Peace and Coroners, and that, with Jerome Hawley and Thomas Cornwallis, councillors who came out with him, he issued an order to encourage emigration by offers of land. The colonists were soon assembled, once within, the very year in which they arrived, as is stated in Chalmer's Annals, for the purpose of legislation and police, secured to them by the charter ; but there are no copies of their laws and very imperfect notes of their proceedings, for the first three or four years. It may now appear strange, but the first difficulty was, where the making of laws should commence ; yet, such has often been the effect of the use of terms like those of the charter, wherein Lord Baltimore was to make laws, "*of and with the advice, assent and approbation*" of the freemen. Those that were forwarded by the proprietary, were rejected by the Assembly ; those drawn up by that body, were refused by him, and the Assembly persisted until they succeeded.

From the list contained in Mr. Bacon's collection, it appears that the latter included bills for swearing allegiance, for the liberties of the people, for laying out church glebes and for the support of the proprietary. The Assembly also were obliged, for want of established laws and courts of justice, to try an agent of Clayborne's, of the name of Thomas Smith, whom they had taken after a combat of pinnaces in the bay, in which some lives on both sides were lost, and condemned as a pirate, passing a bill of attainder against his principal, then gone to England to seek in vain that redress which, however unwillingly, the government of Virginia had been obliged to refuse him. Assemblies were composed of the Governor, as President, Jerome Hawley, Thomas Cornwallis and John Lewger, Esqs. his councillors, summoned by writs of the Governor; as were the chief officers of the province, for some years; sitting as individuals in their own rights, and also as proxies for some others, and all the freemen who should chuse to attend; and all were freemen, except hirelings, paupers and servants. The number of votes with the proxies, about seventy. Mr. Lewger, who had lately arrived, was also appointed by the proprietary, Collector, Treasurer and Secretary of the province, and acted as such to the Assembly, and Surveyor-general, Judge in causes testamentary and conservator of the peace by the Governor, who also appointed him his deputy, when absent in 1638, but was by him suspended for a short time, for committing to Captain Fleete, extravagant and unlawful authority. When reappointed, he was also made attorney-general. Captain Robert Wintour, then lately arrived, was made a Councillor early in the year, and in the course of the summer Mr. Hawley died.

Among the acts passed at a Session held at St. Mary's, five years after they arrived in the country, that is, 1639, we find the first relating to the House of Assembly itself. Here, upon writs being issued by the Governor, delegates elected by the freemen were to sit as burgesses, one or two for each hundred, with the persons specially called by the Governor, and such freemen as had not consented to the election of others, or any twelve or more of them, including always the Governor and Secretary. Their Acts being assented to by the Governor, were to be as binding as if the proprietary and all the freemen had been present, until assented to or rejected by him: and it was intended that those Assemblies should be called once in three years, at least, as it is believed.

After providing that the Governor should hold courts of justice, and the Secretary take probats of wills, they proceeded to extend a limited jurisdiction to the commander of Kent, who was Captain George Evelyn; some of its original settlers submitting willingly. Tobacco planters were required to plant corn also. The debts due the proprietary were to be preferred, and none for wine or spirit, to be recovered until all others were discharged; swearing all to administer justice according to the laws or laudable usages of this province when provided, and renewing the rights of all as English born subjects, according to the great charter of England; establishing the trial by jury of twelve freemen at least, after indictment, in criminal cases. The Governor had with Captain Robert Wintour and John Lewger, held a county court at St. Mary's, in which a grand jury presented Clayborne and Smith to the Assembly, and Thomas Baldridge was appointed Sheriff and Coroner, for one year. County Courts rose with the counties, in the persons of the commander and commissioners, their powers and jurisdiction being very limited, with appeals to the provincial court, which consisted of the Governor and Council, at that time, as well as from the Governor, as Chancellor. It is stated in manuscript notes obligingly communicated by T. Harris, Esq. clerk of the Court of Appeals, that it was a practice to hold the Provincial Court at different places, and also, for one of the council to be placed at the head of the commission for the county courts, for some time, as commander of such county.

There were certain powers given to the captain of the military band, then probably Mr. Cornwallis, who had captured Smith, and was the Governor's deputy during some absences; and a Treasurer, who was Mr. Giles Brent, then made a member of the council also, was to pay all the public charges on the order of the Governor and Council. These were first raised by a duty of five pounds in one hundred of all tobacco exported except to England, Ireland and Virginia; and not exceeding twenty thousand pounds were voted for the erection of a *water-mill*, to be levied on all the inhabitants, as the Governor and Council should direct.

Thus an article of which it was once endeavoured to prevent the consumption in the parent country, became the medium staple here instead of wheat or money, in so short a time; and although its importation from other countries was prohibited there, this source of revenue must have diminished greatly, when that government interdicted the direct trade from the colonies to other countries. From the impost thus levied, it is to be concluded, that such interdictions of trade in the staple, were not anticipated by the colonists and they were never willingly assented to by them or by the proprietaries, as will be seen hereafter.

The cultivation of tobacco appears to have been accompanied by, if it did not produce the introduction of slavery in Maryland, negroes being already the labourers of other colonies, where that or sugar was planted; and, it was at this early day thought necessary by some, to deprive them of a full and equal enjoyment of the privileges or protection of the laws, as appears by one amongst a number of bills presented to this Assembly on different subjects, which however were not finally acted on or passed, at that time at least.

In 1640, owing probably, to the obstructed intercourse with the, natives and the necessity of providing stores for the military, the exportation of corn was prohibited; and three viewers or inspectors of tobacco were to be appointed by the commander in every hundred, sometimes co-extensive with a county. When a hogshead should be found to contain *bad* tobacco for the greater part, it was to be burned, and when not sealed for *good*, the exportation was prohibited under treble damages: It was however not uncommon, even at a later period, to ship that article in bulk as we now do staves or other lumber. It was provided also, that in case of the death of the Governor, the first named of the council should act in his place until a new one was appointed by the proprietary.

The next year one subsidy of fifteen pounds of tobacco per poll was granted the proprietary for the maintenance of the government; and to contribute to this, every inhabitant male or female, except children under twelve years of age, were bound; a system of taxation perhaps equal in the infancy of the colony, when there had been little or no visible property acquired except lands, and every persons means were necessarily dependent on the quantity of labour at his disposal; accordingly, we find that fugitives were punished with forfeiture of life unless pardoned by the Governor.

Encouragement was given to the English and Irish only, and in 1641, they were to bring in arms and amunition, according to Lord Baltimore's *conditions of plantation;* the quit rents being also raised to two shillings sterling for one hundred acres yearly; which was the rate established in Virginia by the crown in 1625; and John Langford, Esq. was appointed Surveyor-general in the place of Mr. Lewger, and for life, because perhaps, a person qualified for such an office, could not be induced to relinquish the emoluments of an established country for the hazards of an infant colony on common terms, and he had probably rendered great services as high-constable of Kent in 1738, but it is the only instance of such tenure. Colonel Francis Trafford, William Blount, Esq. and this gentleman were also made councillors on the resignation of Mr. Cornwallis in 1642; and all these officers appointed during pleasure, were generally re-appointed or continued as long as they lived. Provision was also made in the same Session, for the appointment of a person or persons to take probats of wills, grant letters of administration and hear testamentary causes in the county or counties, and most of this authority was vested in each county court, with appeal to the provincial court or Governor and council, for some years. But the original jurisdiction of the county courts was much restricted, both in criminal and civil cases, until a few years before the province became independant.

In 1642 an act was passed for "an expedition against the Indians," which indicates the approaching difficulties of the colony at the time. Indeed it seems that in this very year some of the Marylanders, who had got amongst the Swedes as far north as the Schuylkill, were attacked by the Dutch, who were sent by Kieft from New-York, by the natives called Manhattan, and by the Dutch New-Amsterdam, claiming the Hudson and Delaware, with the lands on both sides of those rivers, which country they called New-Netherlands. They excited the Indians, took forcible possession and drove our colonists back on the Chesapeake. Within eight years after their arrival, in less time than either south or north Virginia had any Assembly, and when the Parliament of England was reducing the power of the peers, the freemen of Maryland formally requested that the burgesses might form a separate house, having a negative in all laws ; but it was not assented to by the Proprietary or carried into effect until 1649.

The Governor going to England in 1643, deputed Giles Brent, Esq. the Treasurer to be his deputy ; to whom the proprietary himself announced his approbation and his own intention to visit the province at an early period, but was prevented by the approaches of the revolution there probably, and never did accomplish it.

The proprietary's benefactor, king Charles, having now been driven from London by the commons, they passed an ordinance offering certain exemptions from customs in England, if the colonists would refuse to employ any other ships but theirs ; which was the foundation of the navigation act and others leading to resistance and American independence. Clayborne who was perhaps already an associate of Cromwell, Hazlerigg and others, who were prevented from leaving England in 1638 by a general order of the government against disorderly fugitives, and now at least a partisan of the commons, instigated a rebellion in the province, to which the Governor returned in 1644.

At the head of the insurgents at this time, was a captain Richard Ingle, and they succeeded in driving Governor Calvert across the Patomack into Virginia, taking St. Mary's and the public records, which were never recovered, and leaves us ignorant of many particulars relating to that eventful time. The Governor however returned and held assemblies in December 1646 and January 1647, when provision was made for repairing Piscataway Fort, which was one of the last public acts of his life, as he embarked for England the latter year and there died.

It appears that in 1644, William Brainthwaite, Esq. was to be Governor during any absence he might make, but that while in Virginia in 1346, the Governor sent a commission of deputy to Captain Richard Hill, and in his last illness in 1647, he appointed Thomas Greene, Esq. who was a member of the council, verbally. This being contested by Capt. Hill, the council decided in favor of Mr. Greene, which was approved by the proprietary, and all Hill's acts made void, because he was not a member of council at the time he was commissioned.

In 1648 (new style) an Assembly was held under Mr. Greene, in which an act was passed for settling the government, "as the present state of things will permit," a title very evincive of the distresses of the time. It is stated by Mr. Kilty, that Mrs. Margaret Brent, a connexion and perhaps heiress of the deputy Governor of that name, who was now attorney for the proprietary, and administratrix of Leonard, just deceased, claimed a voice in the Assembly, by proxy we presume, and being refused by Mr. Greene, made a formal protest against their proceedings.

The office of Surveyor-general, being vacant by the death of Mr. Langford, Robert Clarke, Esq. was appointed in his place and made a member of Council. It was from this time, that deputy-surveyors as well as deputy-commissaries of wills, were appointed for each county, the latter by their principals, but the former were often by the Governors or Proprietaries.

Mr. Greene who had less discretion or foresight than his employer, proclaimed Charles II. and was succeeded the next year on this account ostensibly, though related to the Proprietary, by Wm. Stone, Esq. and now the Assembly appear to have sat in two distinct houses. It was in this Assembly, under the title of, "an act concerning religion," that liberty of conscience, was established, if it had not been before, by prohibiting, under severe penalties, any molestation of, "persons professing to believe in Jesus Christ, for, or in respect of, his or her religion, or the free exercise thereof." That this liberality did not proceed from fear of others on the one hand, or licentious dispositions in the government on the other, is sufficiently evident, from the penalties prescribed against blasphemy, swearing, drunkenness and Sabbath-breaking, by the preceeding sections of the act, and proviso at the end, that such exercise of religion did not molest or conspire against the Proprietary or his government. Viewing the situation of the colony, it was good policy no doubt, even towards the dissenters, under whose extreme severity, all others, except perhaps the Jews, enjoyed a greater liberty of conscience in the parent country than the Roman Catholics.

The same laudable spirit induced the Assembly to pass an act under a title equally concise of, "an act touching Indians," by which it was felony of death, to take, entice, surprise, transport or sell any friendly Indian, but the felony of death was without forfeiture of estate and according to modern jurisprudence. The people were also prohibited from selling guns or ammunition to Indians, or purchasing their lands, without authority derived from the Proprietary. An assessment was to be raised on all the inhabitants to replace his stock of cattle taken for the army, and a further duty of ten shillings per hogshead granted him on all tobacco exported in Dutch vessels for seven years, to be collected before shipping, by the Governor; one half of which was however, to be employed yearly towards discharging the debts incurred in recovering and defending the province. The good will which the colonists professed towards the Proprietary in this gift during their "distracted condition," may be appreciated, when we consider that it was necessary to pass "an order providing for the relief of the poor," the year after, when the colony did not probably contain a thousand freemen.

At the Assembly of this year, 1649, the Proprietary having acceded to the views of the burgesses, the councillors and they sat in different houses, and the titles of their *acts* were changed accordingly.

Encouragement was now offered to settlers from all countries, but they were enjoined to take an oath of fidelity to the Proprietary, who forbad all grants in trust or to corporate bodies; a system which he reprobated, because perhaps, he had noticed abuses in the Virginia and Plymouth Companies.

The Assembly of 1650, proceeded formally to divide themselves into two houses by law. There were eleven members of the upper-house, including the Governor, viz: Wm. Stone, Jas. Neale, Thomas Greene, Wm. Brainthwaite, John Price, Thomas Hatton, Jno. Pile, Robert Clarke, Robert Brooke, Wm. Eltonhead and Wm. Mitchell, Esquires, and eleven burgesses from six hundreds in St. Mary's county, viz: Messrs. John Hatch, Walter Beane, John Medley, Wm. Broughe, Robert Robins, Francis Posie, Philip Land, Francis Brooke, Thos. Matthews, Thos. Sterman and George Manners; one from Kent Island, who was Robert Vaughan, the commander, and two from *Providence*, Messrs. George Puddington and James Cox, which they immediately erected into a county by the name of Anne Arundal

Here were a government of checks and balances already; legislative powers divided and derived from different sources, very independent, preventing combinations or cabals, and securing to the laws, in their formation as well as in their execution, the utmost deliberation and disinterestedness of which civil society is susceptible, at least as far as then discovered.

By the act for settling the Assembly and, "for the more convenient dispatch of the business" the Governor and Secretary, or any one or more of the council, should be the upper-house, and the fourteen burgesses, by name, or any five of them, the lower-house, and all bills assented to by the major part of them, enacted and published by the Governor, should be laws of the province, as fully as if advised and assented to by all the free-men personally. It was for some time the practice of the Governor to sit and preside in the Assembly or the upper-house, but he still retained a negative; and though he was empowered to assent to laws on the part of the Proprietary, the latter retained and exercised his negative also; but, while the proprietary Government existed, the laws, or *acts,* were not submitted to the government of England or any branch of it, unless from discretion. When in the province, the Proprietary superceded the Governor and occupied his seat, and though he generally appointed all the councillors and high officers, they were sometimes appointed by the Governors. Such continued to be the form of government of Maryland, with little variation, and except during the revolutions of the parent country, while it remained a domain of Lord Baltimore and his heirs.

The two houses, after the burgesses had chosen James Cox, Esq. one of the deputies from Anne Arundel, their speaker, the Governor appointing Mr. Wm. Bretton, clerk, passed a most humble act of recognition to the Proprietary, as the *first fruits* of their fidelity and thankfulness. While they accompanied this declaration with an act for the speedy payment of his debts and the reservation of the deserted plantations; they prohibited the raising of money or waging of war abroad without their consent, as well as all compliance with Clayborne: they also passed an act of oblivion, with an exception of Ingle and another. Although it was the practice with the natives to put their prisoners to death generally, it was not always the case, and a levy was made for redeeming two orphans detained by them; and it seems some red people were kept as hostages or servants by individuals, in spite of laws; but then the Assembly ordered a march upon the Indians, the re-edifying the fort at St. Inagoes, which in fact was their immediate dwelling, and provided for the registering of marriages, births and burials.

The Parliament of London laid a specific duty of three pence per pound on tobacco, which was increased at this time considerably and imitated by that at Oxford. The order which was issued by the Parliament this year, for prohibiting trade with Virginia and several West India islands, must have increased the difficulties of our colonists who participated in the loyalty which was the cause of it, and they were not lessened by a similar act of Massachusetts soon after, when the famous navigation act was produced; both of them to secure the commerce and reduce the southern colonies to compliance with the Parliament. Thus were the troubles of Maryland caused by the English colonists of America or English factionists at home, and no evidence appears that the parent country gave any assistance to our ancestors, either in procuring the soil she granted or settling their internal government: which, if bound at all by those charters, considered preposterous as mere donations of foreign territories, she should have done; nor could the obligation be dissolved by domestic difficulties of her own creation which may have prevented her interference. She will scarcely find a justification for the regulation of the trade of the colonies thus commenced, in her opposition to the encroachments upon them by rival nations, or upon one another by the different Proprietaries, as she sometimes did, both before and after the grant of Maryland, for she commenced and terminated her disputes with them at her own discretion, and not always to the advantage of the colonists or the Proprietaries.

Those measures giving sanction to the reformers here, appear to have had the effect of dividing our colonists; and the parties took up arms against each other, so that Governor Stone was obliged to abandon the administration of civil affairs to command the loyalists. What battles they fought, and how many were killed is unknown to us, but these painful broils, although confined to so small a territory, for there were still Indian towns on the Patuxent, gave the rival neighbours time and opportunity to fortify themselves and create future difficulties to the Proprietary and the province. Sweden had done little for her colonists and they remained quiet at Tinicum Island, when in 1651, the Dutch landed at New-Castle and built a fort there, by which the Swedes were alarmed, and Rizing, retook it and erected another fort at Christeen for their further security.

It appears that Messrs. Francis Yardley, Rich'd Preston and Richard Banks were added to the number of councillors in 1652, when the insurgents subdued Governor Stone, partially at least, and got possession of the province. Clayborne secured the confidence of the ruling party by his hostility to the Proprietary's government, and was now with Capt. Dennis and two others, commissioned for "reducing, settling and governing all the plantations within the bay of the Chesapeake." They forced Governor Berkely to deliver up the colony of Virginia, as a domain of the crown, but not without some fighting and a capitulation. Governer Stone was not displaced directly, but required to govern in the name of the Lord Protector, which Lord Baltimore resisted of course. The colonists again embodied under Mr. Stone and resisted, and so far succeeded, that the Governor and council erected a new county, which they called Calvert; but the parties were very unequal, especially after the reduction of Virginia, and finally, in 1654, Cromwell's commissioners landed and assembled their forces on the *north side* of the Patuxent, where the people appear to have been more favorable to them than those of St. Mary's, and compelled the Governor to submit. The victors issued a commission to Capt. Wm. Fuller, Richard Preston, who was one of the council, Edward Lloyd, who had been commander of Anne Arundal seven years before, William Durand, who was made Secretary by the others, John Smith, Leonard Strong, John Lawson, John Hatch, Richard Wells and Richard Ewen, to be Governors and judges, under Cromwell, and took and tried Governor Stone by a court-martial, and he was condemned to be shot; but he had endeared himself even to the soldiery so much, that they dared not take his life, and he remained a long time in confinement.

In the mean time an expedition was sent from England under Nicholls, with which the northern colonists were pressed to join, to expel the Dutch from New-Netherlands, but little aid was given and the object failed. An Assembly was held under this commission at Patuxent, for the new Governors abolished the name of Calvert county as they had that of Anne Arundel, in which the upper-house was done away. Messrs. Thomas Hatton and Job Chandler who were burgesses for St. Mary's county, refused to serve, as being inconsistent with the oath they had taken to Lord Baltimore, but two others were returned in their places; Mr. Hatton had been a member of council, Secretary, Commissary and Attorney-general; the first appointed after Mr. Lewger, and Mr. Chandler had been also a member of council. The oath of fidelity was repealed and the exercise of the Roman Catholic religion restrained, declaring that none who professed it should be protected either by the laws of the kingdom or of the commonwealth. Such laws were passed as would protect other sects, except Episcopalians, who were prohibited from prelacy or government by bishops, &c. and tendering the lands to emigrants on the original conditions. The terms of Assemblies were now fixed at three years.

It seems that the Virginians wanted again to renew their claims to Maryland during these troublesome times; at least the parliament commissioners charged Lord Baltimore with going to the King at Oxford and having commanded Stone's opposition to their authority; wishing themselves to annex this province to that which they governed, as may be seen in Thurlor's state papers; but Cromwell, who knew how to divide and reign, by letters to his Governors in 1655 and 1656 interposed his authority; nor would he suffer the disputes of the Swedes and Dutch on the northern frontier to disturb the pacific policy he had now determined to maintain towards those powers, while he was extending the British dominions in the West Indies at the expense of Spain. It was at this period that New-Castle and Christeen changed masters, being taken from Rizing the Swedish Governor, by Stuyvesant the Governor of New-Netherlands.

Then too, there arose in Maryland an individual who resembled the Protector, in dissimulation if not in courage, called

Josias Fendall, who gave his commissioners much trouble and had mainly contributed to the late civil wars, the dangers of which, one might think, would outweigh any personal advantage he could expect from them. After holding one other Assembly in 1657, in which was passed an act of recognition; and laying an assessment of thirty-two pounds of tobacco per poll, to defray the expenses of Fendall's war, and other charges; the commissioners surrendered the government to this man, who had intrigued or manœuvred so well as to be trusted with a commission from Lord Baltimore. Fendall in fact summoned together the two houses of Assembly in 1658, to meet at St. Leonards, having created a new county which he named Charles, as a compliment to the future King or Proprietary, for that was the name of Cecilius' son, and before the death of Cromwell, in which a few laws of ordinary import were passed; he also held a provincial court, Philip Calvert, Esq. a brother of the Proprietary, being Secretary and Richard Smith, Esq. Attorney-general; whose decisions are the first reported by Harris and M'Henry; but, in 1659 the Assembly were called together at Thomas Gerrard's, to dissolve the upper-house. The Governor, pressed by Thomas Slye, Esq. the speaker, who had been one of Cromwell's commissioners four years before the above Thomas Gerrard, though he had been a councillor under Brent and Stone, and colonel Nathaniel Utie, who had been made one in 1658 by Fendall himself, under instructions from the Proprietary to him, gave it as his opinion, that the charter invested the power of making laws in the burgesses only. After joining with them, he accepted a new commission from them as Governor; and, new modelled like the commonwealth of England, they with his consent repealed all former acts, disguising the treachery to the proprietary, under a feigned loyalty to the King whose restoration they anticipated, and whose dominion they would probably have preferred. The councillors or members of the upper-house, who protested and did not, like the three last mentioned, take seats in the other house, were the late Governor Stone, Secretary Calvert, colonel John Price, Job Chandler, Robert Clarke, Baker Brooke, who was a nephew of the Proprietary, Edward Lloyd, esquires, and Doctor

Luke Barber, whom Fendall himself had during a late absence, made his deputy. The Governor however exerted the force of the colony to maintain its limits against the Dutch, and sent colonel Utie to New-Castle to warn them away. Utie who was re-appointed councillor by the Proprietary, and more of a soldier perhaps than politician, took up land in Baltimore county, which was then first erected; whether by law or by order of the Governor, does not appear, but was represented in the Assembly the same year, and is sufficient evidence of the fact. Counties were created sometimes by a proclamation of the Governor, but it seems that the appointment of commissioners or justices, was alone sufficient in some instances, and was probably the case as to this county.

Immmediately after Charles the second was restored, the Proprietary appointed his brother and late Secretary of the province, Philip Calvert, Esq. to be Governor, accompanied with instructions from the King, "to all officers and subjects, to be aiding in the re-establishment of his lordship's just *rights and jurisdictions.*" The Proprietary also obtained by decision of commissioners in England, a confirmation of his father's patent for Avalon, which had been granted to the Marquis of Hamilton and others, at the commencement of the civil war.

Baker Brooke, John Bateman, Robert Clarke, and Edward Lloyd, esquires, were councillors; Henry Coursey, esq. councillor, secretary and commissary, Thos. Manning, esq. was attorney-general, and Mr. Brooke succeeded Mr. Clarke as surveyor-general. By his own instructions, the quit rents and alienation fines were fixed at four shillings sterling, per one hundred acres yearly, for the former; and though the rents were fixed in money only, his agents were at liberty to take wheat or other produce at a fair price, as the contracts stipulated for a long time, and he occasionally accepted of the old or half rents of two shillings.

Fendall and Gerrard were condemned to be banished, but having surrendered themselves, the punishment was changed to fine and disqualification to office; a lenity which, in this instance, as in others to be found in our history, was paid by future treacherous and ungrateful acts.

The former privileges of the colony were renewed, as fully as if the Proprietary had suffered no privations in England, or his Catholic brethren no persecutions in Maryland; and the Governor assembled the two houses early in 1661. The very first act they passed, and perhaps the first of the kind in America, was to provide a public maintainance for those who should be maimed in defence of their country. There was immediate necessity for levies, to quell the Indians, called Janadoas, probably from the country beyond the Patowmack, about the Shenandoah, and the governor was authorised to call in the aid of the Susquehannahs; which in our ancestors, was not a policy dictated by ambition, but a necessary resort for safety from savage nations which must have overpowered them if united, and no doubt a principal means of their triumph over unequal numbers. Further to relieve the trade of the country, a mint was established, and the only one on the continent except in Massachusetts, where it was objected to by the crown, as an encroachment on its prerogative. Here shillings were to be coined, containing at least nine pence worth of sterling silver; not from mines, which our ancestors never sought, but from the fruits of their industry; which were to be put into circulation in return for tobacco, at two pence per pound, and thus the currency was fixed as it continued until the war of independence, at 6s. for a dollar, or 133 1-3 per cent sterling. The British nation were so much gratified with the abolition of certain feudal or military tenures personally degrading, by the reformers, that the King gave his assent to an act for its ratification, and he disliked the Dutch, who, until that time, maintained the greatest trade with the province; but the acts of the English Parliament, revived or lately enacted, prohibiting the exportation of the staple articles, such as sugar, tobacco, cotton, indigo, &c. from the colonies to, or the importation of any articles from any foreign dominions; confining all the trade and navigation to British subjects, which, it is true, was admitted to include the colonists, excepting only the ports of India and within the straights; and subjecting the imports from the colonies into England, and the exports into them from thence, to a shilling in the pound value, were so many instances of the readiness of the Commons and the King to continue the measures the late government, where policy or interest seemed to sanction or require it. With a due sense of their interests, if not power to enforce their rights as Englishmen and parties in the empire, entitled to trade every where under proper regulations; the government of Maryland retaliated by the establishment of port or anchorage duties, which were to be paid the Proprietary, of half a pound of powder and three pounds of shot, or so much in value, for every ton of burthen of "all vessels, whatsoever not properly belonging to this province, having a deck flush fore and aft, coming in and trading."

As a further proof of the interest Lord Baltimore took in the colony, he sent out his only son, Charles, to be Governor in 1662; and who though a youth, appeared to have inherited the energy as well as the virtues of his father.

The late Governor Calvert was appointed deputy Governor and chancellor; and except in two or three instances afterwards, the only case where that office was separated from the Governor, or Governor and councillors for the time being. It being also of the first importance to have men of talent in such an office, the Proprietary appointed Mr. Jerome White surveyor-general, with instructions to lay off two or three hundred acres of land, which were to be in St. Mary's, at the usual quit rent, for the express purpose of planting vines, some wine having been already made in Virginia before the establishment of our colony; but fashion and private interest prevailed over public utility in both, and tobacco continued to be the principal or only staple. Mr. White who was to have the vineyard, was also made a member of council afterwards.

By one of the first acts under the administration of the new Governor it was declared that, where the laws of the province had not otherwise provided, justice should be administered according to the statutes and practice in England; which though it was a mere revival of one of the first of the provincial laws, produced *an act of gratitude,* providing twenty-five pounds of tobacco per poll for his own use, and which was continued annually as long as his father lived. It was more common afterwards, and under all the different administrations, to allow the

Governor three pence a hogshead on Tobacco exported, in addition to such salaries as were granted by the government. Provision was made for the appointment of a Coroner in each county by the Executive, who also appointed the Sheriffs, which officer with the commissioners held the elections, and the latter appointed the constables. The Governor prepared an expedition against the Dutch settlement at the *Hoarkill*, now called Lewistown, where they had levied duties on the trade of the Delaware, but which those people, anticipating the fate of their colony and yielding to the solicitations of the Proprietary himself with Holland, abandoned on his son's approach; and Beckman the Dutch Governor, received and entertained our Governor at New-Castle. Particular encouragement was given to such as should take up lands and settle in the neighborhood of Lewistown, under our Proprietary, to secure the possesion no doubt. Parliament entirely suppressed the growth of tobacco in England and permitted the colonists to import salt and Madeira wine direct in 1763.

Although patents were granted for lands in Baltimore county to Colonel Utie and others, during Fendall's administration in 1759, it was immediately represented in Assembly, and courts were held in it two years after, to pass those titles, "An act for seating of lands in Baltimore county," introduced in 1664, was rejected by the Proprietary; probably because he judged the extension of the then settlements on the west side of the bay premature while there was danger from enemies at home or abroad. But an act for quieting possessions and enrolling conveyances was duly sanctioned, and so were others for the encouragement of trade and manufactures; one for instance, for preserving the harbours and another to prevent the exportation of wool. Colonel Utie and Colonel William Evans were appointed councillors, and Wm. Calvert, Esq. a nephew of the Proprietary, attorney-general, and afterwards commissary-general, being the first commission in which this office was taken from the Secretary,

Another expedition was sent from England to New-Netherlands to expel the Dutch, and Stuyvesant surrended the colony to Colonel Nicolls; and the whole remaining to England by the treaty of peace in 1667, was granted to the Duke of York, which finally deprived Lord Baltimore of the lands bordering on this side of the Delaware, from its mouth to Philadelphia. By the treaty of Breda, each party retained its conquests, and the Dutch having taken Surinam, got out of a neighborhood which they had found troublesome, on advatageous terms.

In 1665, the Proprietary gave his son, then Governor, and his male heirs, a reversion cf almost all his manors and directed more to be laid off for him.

In 1666, an act was passed authorising the Governor and council to make war or peace with hostile Indians, and another to prohibit the planting of tobacco for one year; not as was contemplated in England in James' reign, to prevent the use of it, but to raise the value; for the article, which on its first introduction and for some time after, sustained the price of six and eight shillings sterling per pound, was now passed in payment here at 6s. per 100. It appears that the quantity already produced so far exceeded the demand, that, in Virginia, the growth was also prohibited and the number of negroes was considered a grievance; it was scarcely less so to persist in a culture which cleared and rendered sterile the uplands while the low and fertile vallies were reserved for the sake of timber, no otherwise cultivated then or since; but Lord Baltimore disapproved of a measure so much like self-destruction, and declared the proposed act would be injurious to the people as well as to the revenues from the customs. Many of the Puritans had emigrated from Virginia, where they were persecuted by the Episcopalians, and people of that and other sects from N. England, where the Puritans persecuted them. It appears too that the people called Quakers, resorted to Maryland for protection, before a refuge was prepared for them in Jersey or Pennsylvania, being better received here than either in *south* or *north Virginia;* but this colony acquired new accessions of Swedes and Dutch, disturbed in their settlements first by the contests among themselves and afterwards by the hostilities of the British and the Dutch about the New-Netherlands. Emigrants also arrived from the continent of Europe disturbed by the revolutions in Portugal and the Netherlands and Lewis XIV's. proscription of Protestants. The acts of naturalization passed this year, were certainly among the first of the kind passed in any of the colonies, and we find the names of families then or soon after naturalized, still familiar in some parts of Maryland; such as Van Swearingen, Lockerman, Van Bibber, Hesselius, Comegys, Le Compte, Maynadier, &c. though the British government would not allow those acts to convey any of the rights or privileges of British subjects out of the colony; and so it was admitted here afterwards; yet it soon fell out with the Catholics of Maryland, as it had done with the Quakers in Pennsylvania, since their liberal policy brought them to be the minority of the people and the government fell from their hands. The governor and council erected a new county by the name of Somerset, and it is thought Dorchester also, though the latter was not represented in the assembly until three years after.

The division line from Watkin's Point across the peninsula to the sea, was fixed in 1668, by Philip Calvert, Esq. and a commissioner from Virginia: but the line on the west is that settled by treaty with the Indians, in 1744.

In 1669 persons desirous of erecting grist-mills were permitted to take up seats of twenty acres on either side of a stream, by valuation of juries, and hold the same eighty years; the tolls being fixed at one eighth of the bushel of wheat and one sixth of the corn; such at least were the terms prescribed by the act of 1704, which from the title appears to be a similar act. Acts were also passed making tobacco a legal tender for money debts, making highways, limiting ordinary or tavern-keepers and providing freight for the proprietary's and governor's tobacco and other goods. A grant of lands was made by act of assembly to the *confederate* Indians of Choptank, and, in 1698, other lands were granted to the Nanticoke Indians in the same neighborhood, on leases of a few beaver skins annually; in the first instance, to them and their heirs forever, but in the latter instance, to them and their heirs and successors forever, or so long as they shall occupy and live upon the same, and confirmed by succeeding laws.

In 1669, the proprietary determined that those only then arrived, and settlers on the Delaware, should have lands at 2s. per 100 acres, others to pay at the rate of four shillings. In this year the governor appointed his uncle Philip Calvert, his cousin William Calvert, and Messrs. White and Brooke, his deputies, paid a visit to his father in England, and was absent the ensuing year.

In 1771, the proprietary directed two manors of six thousand acres each, to be laid off and reserved in each county, where it had not been done; a part of which was to be at the disposal of his *son and heir*, Charles, the governor. The assembly repealed the acts for the support of the proprietary of 1649 and 1650, it being intended to raise supplies by duties on tobacco, accordly two shillings sterling per hogshead was imposed on all tobacco exported; one half to defray the charges of government, and the other for the proprietary, he receiving the quit rents and alienation fines in that article at two pence per pound.

This was to be collected during his life, but was afterwards re-enacted for the life of his son Charles and grandson Cecilius. As the price of the article varied, it is evident the value of the grant varied also; the proprietary received less than his rent at one time and more at another, so that after many disputes on this subject, money was alone paid at last by offer of the assembly itself, but the vague terms used caused much of the difficulty. Acts were also passed to establish a standard of weights and measures, which fortunately for the colonists generally, was taken by all from one English standard, and is therefore of great facility in their commercial intercourse; to encourage the growth of hemp and flax; to establish rates for the sale of goods by retail, foreign *engrossers* being proscribed before. The importation of negroes was also encouraged; for it was said, there were still a greater number of servants than slaves in the province.

There appears to have been no meeting of the assembly from this time during two or three years; and it was possibly, because the parliament had undertaken to make laws for the colonists, as disagreeable to the proprietary and governor as to them. The regulations to which the ministry subjected the colonies, under the navigation acts or otherwise, had produced new appeals from their authority to the house of commons, and the nation having just gone to war, parliament took the opportunity to draw new aids from settlements which they now deemed fixed if not wealthy, by taxing the products on their exportation, though it was contrary to the express terms of the twentieth article of the charter. Tobacco for instance, by an act of 1662, might be sent to some foreign countries, but going there, was to pay a certain duty at the place of shipment; if no duty was to be paid, bonds were to be given to unlade in England, Ireland or the colonies; the commissioners of customs in England were to appoint the collectors of this duty, and provision was made for taxing oil and fins imported into England in colonial ships, while such importations in British ships were exempt. No legislative act was passed here to enforce the duties at the time; but, by the appointment of the governor himself, as agent for the commissioners, the collection was at least partially effected through his address and vigilance; and with a view of preventing the exactions of strangers in office perhaps, he continued collector of these duties until he became proprietary of the colony himself.

A Mr. Jones and other Marylanders, took possession of Lewistown and plundered the British officers fixed there by the government of New-York; of which Mr. Lovelace, the governor of that province, addressed a serious remonstrance to our deputy governor, Philip Calvert, esquire, immediately; the effect of which is unknown to us.

There was at this time a prerogative court, in which the chancellor presided, but the commissary-general continued to appoint deputies in the counties,

In 1673, lord Baltimore authorised the leasing of his manor lands, except about one tenth of each for a mansion, for terms of years not exceeding thirty, or three lives; fixing the rents thereof at the price of the quit rents generally, with a condition of clearing, enclosing, planting an orchard, &c. and a small fee or alienation fine, continued to be collected on sales, though not always on devises, during the proprietary government.

In 1674, the governor returned and created a new county, which he named after his father Cecil, for Cecilius. Provision was made by law for erecting a state-house and prison at St. Mary's, as well as a court-house and prison in each county, and for subsidizing the Susquehanna Indians, against the Senecas. The latter are stated to have had one thousand fighting men, and two thousand one hundred and fifty with the Mohawks and others, excited to partake in hostilities by the Dutch admiral Binkes, who recovered New-York from Manning the deputy-comandant, the year before; but peace being made again at the very time governor Calvert had prepared an expedition against them at Lewistown, the whole was restored this year to sir Edmond Andross and remained in the hands of the English by treaty; as that of 1667, secured to the parties their respective conquests, and this, the restoration of conquests on either side.

By the death of Cecilius on the 30th of November, 1675, the titles and estates of Lord Baltimore, descended to his son Charles, then governor of Maryland. The late Lord Baltimore was about seventy-three years old when he died; his mother was Anne, daughter of George Mynne, esq. of Hertingfordbury in Hertfordshire, and his lady was Anne, daughter of Thomas Arundel, Earl of Arundel of Wardour, and Count of the Holy Roman Empire.

The new proprietary called an assembly for the purpose of revising all the laws, confirming and rendering many salutary ones *perpetual*, while the new ones could be immediately sanctioned by his presence in the colony. Among the latter, we find acts for the recovery of small debts and limitations of officers fees; against the exportation of corn and the importation of convicts, then becoming the practice of the British government, but uniformly and earnestly opposed here. After providing for the defence of the colonists by a new organization of the militia, he left the province under the nominal government of his infant son Cecilius, but virtually under his deputy, colonel Jesse Wharton, who was president of the council, and returned to England, not so much probably to enjoy any honors which awaited him there, as to defend himself and his interests here.

It is stated that Cecilius, Lord Baltimore, had occupied a seat in the parliament of England before the revolution, but it does not appear that he ever took his seat among the lords in Ireland; that he had expended 40,000*l* sterling in the first establishment of the province, and had even been obliged to take advances in England from some of the colonists, but his protracted life afforded him an opportunity to receive some interest for his money in their affections, if not in actual revenue. During his proprietaryship, which, including the short period of the revolution, the people had explored and partially settled all the shores of the bay; they had many allies among the indians and were never overpowered by any of them alone; they knew their own rights, and generally enjoyed them. A press was maintained in the colony from an early period; which, after the accession of William and Mary, is said by Mr. Chalmers to be the only one; and the most perfect liberty of conscience then legally existing. Though the governor and proprietary were Roman Catholics, there were, it was said, thirty Protestants for one Catholic in the colony at the time of the latter's decease; there was no establishment but glebe lands, nor tythes or stipend for clergymen; an asylum was offered to persons of all sects and nations; there never was but one officer appointed during life, nor any title of nobility created; latterly the proprietary advised his son to recommend some distinction of dress or otherwise, for the governor, judges and officers of the colony, as adopted here afterwards; the judges at this time and previously, wearing only a ribband and medal; having readily abandoned all ideas of feudal establishments in it, if he had ever wished to exercise the powers of the charter in this respect.

In the infancy of the establishment, the people looked up to Lord Baltimore as to a common father, and when their population amounted it is said, to nearly twenty thousand, they continued their acts of *gratitude;* and never, as far as we have discovered, did he complain of the want of it. It is with great justice and truth observed by Doctor Ramsay, in his History of the Revolutionary War, that, "the prosperity of the colony was founded on the broad basis of security to property and freedom in religion, and never," continues this historian in the language of Mr. Chalmers, "did a people enjoy more happiness than the inhabitants of Maryland under Cecilius, the founder of the province."

Colonel Wharton died soon after his appointment of deputy governor, but commissioned Thomas Notley, esq. who had filled that office before, to succeed him. In the mean time, that is in 1676, a devise of real and personal estate made by Mr. Robert Cadger, of St. Mary's, for the maintenance of a Protestant ministry, was, on the representation of the Mayor, Recorder, &c. duly confirmed by act of assembly and by the proprietary, and that corporation made trustee thereof.

In 1677, colonel Coursey, one of the council, and afterwards chief justice of the provincial court, negociated a peace with the Senecas and the rest of the *Five Nations*, at Albany, for Maryland and Virginia. To this confederacy of Indians, was added the Tuscarora's about thirty-five years after, making the *Six Nations*.

In 1678, Edward Husbands, a practitioner of medicine, being charged with an attempt to poison the governor and council, and abusing and cursing the delegates, was ordered by them to be whipped; but he probably escaped the fine which was imposed on him, and the prohibition to practice, by Lord Baltimore's dissent to the act on his return.

In 1680, John Llewellin, esq. was appointed clerk and register of the land office, which was then first separated from the duties of secretary, and both judges and registers were separately appointed at different times, until as last, they were only deputies or clerks. The indulgences which Charles the second was now disposed to show the dissenters produced new intrigues against his government, while it was suspected in parliament, that the king only intended by the changes, to afford more liberty to the Catholics; and, as if to screen themselves, it appears that the ministry listened to some unfounded charges against the proprietary; as, that he promoted the aggrandizement of the Roman priests, and permitted much licentiousness in the people.

The government of Virginia too, had sent complaints that Lord Baltimore had forced them to pay anchorage in the Patowmack, and had not taken his part in opposing the Indians. To the former, which was done by act of assembly, he had a chartered right, if not a natural one, as the river to the south shore was within his limits; and of the rest, he proved their falsehood and absurdity; after which, in 1681, he returned to Maryland, where his presence became more and more necessary, from the same sort of cabal transferred from the parent state to the colony, and which had actually overthrown the royal government in Virginia, where the disaffected were headed by one Nathaniel Bacon, a young lawyer.

The same Josias Fendall, before spoken of, and one John Coode were immediately arrested, presented and tried for sedition: the former was convicted, fined heavily and banished, but the latter was acquitted and lived to foment future disturbances. The proprietary also called two assemblies the same year, where acts were passed to prevent vexatious law-suits, and for bringing criminals to certain and speedy trial; restraining the exportation of leather and raw hides, deer and elk skins, as was expressly declared *for the encouragement of tanners and shoemakers*, and they revised the militia code, in order to afford a stronger defence against the Indians; and thus also to allay the reproaches of the malcontents in the adjoining colony as well as his own province.

In 1682, induced by the same just and pacific policy, acts were passed for the encouragement of tillage and raising provisions; for sowing hemp and flax and making linen and woollen cloths; and, to prevent the exactions of the custom-house officers, country ships were *expressly* exempted from the tonnage duty imposed by the colony, as was also declared by some of the acts.

Mr. Markham, the agent of Wm. Penn, esq. arrived in the Delaware the year before, and had an interview with the proprietary of Maryland, and now the proprietary of Pennsylvania himself waited on him for the purpose of a settlement of limits. Our proprietary received the latter on the *Severn;* but as if etiquette required less, he met the former at Chester on the Delaware, which they discovered to be within Lord Baltimore's lines. Mr. Penn had been one of the Jersey Company, and the duke of York had made him a present of New Castle and twelve miles round, before he obtained a cession of the counties of Kent and Sussex; and in consequence of these acquisitions, he had already written to Messrs. Frisby and Herman, inhabitants of the eastern side of the bay, that they were settled within his province, and must pay their rents and taxes accordingly. In their interviews, the proprietary of Pennsylvania exhibited a letter from the king, which directed *Lord Baltimore* to measure his limits from Watkins' Point on the south, two degrees of sixty miles each only; which of course fell short of the fortieth degree of north latitude; but our proprietary answered, "that a royal mandate could not deprive him of what had been granted under the great seal." With the dignity of character displayed in that language towards his sovereign, he did not hesitate to declare to his immediate opponent and fellow subject, that the king had been imposed upon; and it is not surprising that people who had lived under his government, or on the borders of it, should prefer such a ruler. It seems in fact many did, and colonel George Talbot, a member of council, surveyor general, a deputy governor under B. L. Calvert afterwards, and probably a son of sir William Talbot, who was one of the council, secretary and commissary-general in 1670, went to Philadelphia with instructions to warn Mr. Penn to remove from thence, as within the fortieth degree and the Maryland grant. The difficulty was caused in the first instance, by the inability of Lord Baltimore to dispossess the Swedes, if not by the respect which he owed them as first christian settlers, by his charter or otherwise, or by the want of it in others; and afterwards in ascertaining the exact limits of the Dutch settlements, some references and reservations suggested by our proprietary's agents to prevent a misunderstanding, had been overlooked in the draft of Mr. Penn's charter, though considered as acceeded to by him, when that act was submitted to those agents.

This tenacious gentleman seems to have thought his province not worth having, if there was not an outlet by the Chesapeake as well as by the Delaware, to which our proprietary was as firmly opposed. There was no greater chance of a settlement in England, where both proprietaries soon returned; for the new king, James II. was inclined to annul the charter of Maryland, though owned by a Catholic, while the other proprietary was, preposterously indeed, accused of being a *Jesuit priest*, for the favor he enjoyed; though afterwards, so perplexed by his colonists and his creditors, that he agreed on terms for the sale of

Pennsylvania to queen Anne, as Mr. Proud informs us; nor was the settlement of these proprietary disputes terminated until a little before the independence of both provinces.

In 1683, an assembly was held at a place called *the Ridge*, in Anne Arundel county. In this assembly the first act was passed for laying out towns, entitled "An Act for the advancement of trade." There were to be four towns in St. Mary's, two in Kent, three in Anne Arundel, one of which called the Landing at Proctor's on the Severn, became the seat of government not long after; four in Calvert, three in Charles, four in Talbot, five in Somerset, two in Dorchester, two in Cecil, and two in Baltimore county, none of which towns were to send burgesses to the assembly *until they could pay their expenses* without being chargeable on their respective counties.

Within four years thirty-three new towns were created by the assembly; returned to the city of St. Mary's, as it was then called; three of which towns were within the limits of Baltimore county; but one of them, on Middle River, was discontinued, with others in Charles, Somerset and Worcester afterwards, and none of them exercised the privilege of representation, or became of much importance, except the *landing on Severn*, when it became the seat of government, by the name of Annapolis. The making and unmaking those towns, which, though they were to be ports or places of landing exclusively, was not apparently attended with difficulty, any more than the making and unmaking *post-offices* in our days; especially as the little ground appropriated for them did not much interfere with the culture of the country. It was, however, a circumstance to be regretted in respect to Baltimore, which was afterwards made a town in the same limited manner. There is no doubt but illegal fees had been frequently exacted on the takers up of land, and the proprietary limited the *just purchase* or consideration, at two hundred pounds of tobacco for every one hundred acres, which, when credited on security was called caution money, and other fees of the land office. The caution was increased afterwards but a long credit was given, or it was wholly relinquished as to the lands of the Delaware, and between the Patowmack and the Susquehanna, to the westward, which he said might *be seen without expense*, meaning of a *guard* probably, to which the first settlers were subjected no doubt; and unnecessary in time of peace.

Colonel Henry Coursey was appointed by special commission chief justice, and Thomas Taillor, Vincent Lowe, Henry Darnall, William Digges, William Stevens, William Burgess and Thomas Trueman, esquires, associate justices of the provincial court, when the council ceased to hold original jurisdiction, or to sit as a court of law in the first instance. The number of justices was less or more, and varied according to the discretion of the executive; and the commissions were sometimes joint and sometimes separate.

In 1684, the proprietary returning to England, appointed his son, Benedict Leonard Calvert, a minor, (Cecil being dead) lieutenant-general, and nine persons, viz. colonel Talbot, Thomas Taillor, Vincent Lowe, the surveyor-general, Henry Darnall, William Digges, William Stevens, William Burgess, Nicholas Sewall and John Darnall, esquires, were all made *commissioners general,* and Clement Hill, esq. a *deputy.* In 1685, William Joseph, esq. was president of the council, and of the upper house when assembled afterwards.

The proprietary had considered the bonds required by the late acts of parliament, on the departure of ships after the duties had been paid, an unnecessary grievance, which he declined enforcing, but Mr. Christopher Rousby being appointed collector in his place by the commissioners of trade, exacted them, and the proprietary solicited his recall; this solicitation was not acceeded to, and he was directed to support the demand of the collector, agreeably to the opinion of Mr. Jones, the attorney general, whom it was thought necessary to consult on the occasion. Colonel Talbot had been employed to defend the settlements at the head of the bay, and while engaged with the collector at Patuxent, in procuring funds for the erection of a fort upon or near Christeen, an affray took place between them, in which the latter lost his life. The colonel fled into Virginia, but being taken, tried and convicted of murder, was afterwards pardoned by king James. While the accession of the duke of York to the throne was announced in the province, the proprietary was again followed by allegations of persecuting Protestants, and other less important charges. Desirous to obtain the province, the king threatened him with a dissolution of the charter for obstructing the customs, and he was compelled to indemnify the crown for some loss of revenue from them.

Assemblies were held in 1686 and 1688, under Benedict L. Calvert, and deputy governors, Mr. Joseph, president, where severe laws were passed against usury, and fixing the currency agreeably to the coins, at six shillings the dollar.

James' toleration, allowing Catholics public worship, had become as obnoxious with some here as it was generally in England. As soon as his flight was known, the proprietary's orders to proclaim William and Mary having miscarried, the people of Maryland began to resist the government also, and forming an association, placed the before mentioned John Coode at their head and obtained the fort and government of the deputies by capitulation.

In 1689, commissioners assembled in convention, of which Kenelm Cheseldine, esq. was chosen speaker, in imitation of and pursuant to instructions from that in England. They met again in 1690, and chose George Robothom, esq. their speaker, but they passed no ordinances except to continue the existing laws, and prohibit the export of corn. Lord Baltimore was outlawed in Ireland in 1690, where he never had been, and therefore got his outlawry reversed by king William immediately, as is stated in the London Magazine of June 1768; where it is strangely said, that a Lord Baltimore of the name of *John*, who they call the father of Charles, had followed king James and sat in parliament. Unfortunately too, some of the servants of Mr. Sewall, another member of the council, killed Mr. Payne, Mr. Rousby's successor as collector of the customs, for which they were brought to trial, condemned and executed.

It does not appear that Mr. Main, who succeeded to that office afterwards, encountered any difficulty or opposition, but that both the provincial and royal customs were collected by him. This however, did not prevent the *Protestant interest*, for which James was expelled from England, being transfered to the colony where so great a majority now professed that faith, and this interest was judged more secure under the immediate government of the new king and queen, so that the proprietary was wholly deprived of political power or the administration of public affairs here. For the same, and other causes, especially the religious scruples of the inhabitants to contribute towards the common defence, though urged so to do by the proprietary as Mr. Proud says, Mr. Penn was also deprived of his government during the year 1693, as New-England and Virginia were by Charles I. and Jersey by queen Anne; so that all the proprietary governments on this continent; were at one time or another entirely extinct. The Carolinas and Georgia being taken by George II. none but Maryland and Pennsylvania remained at last.

William and Mary confirmed to Lord Baltimore the whole of the port or tonnage duty lately converted to money at fourteen pence, after a formal decision of council, contrary to the views of the assembly, who said they held Lord Baltimore accountable for the other half received. The new government accordingly forbid the obstructions which had been raised against colonel Henry Darnall, who had been some time a judge and register of the land-office and agent and receiver of rents for Lord Baltimore, and who had been actually imprisoned during the late troubles; the proprietary having doubled the rates of rent, and adopted other means of defence or reprisal; such as, authority to increase the caution money and fees of the land office in proportion to those exacted by the new chancellor and secretary, to which he did not consider them entitled, and which continued to be a subject of long and obstinate dispute, so that the land office was actually closed part of the time that the provincial government was held by the crown.

In 1691, colonel Lionel Copley was appointed captain-general, and Henry Jowles, Nehemiah Blakiston, Nicholas Greenburry, George Robothom, Clarles Hutchins, David Brown, Thomas Tench, John Addison, John Courts, Thomas Brooke and James Frisby, esquires, were his councillors. Sir Thomas Lawrence, Bart. appointed councillor and secretary soon after Mr. Copley's appointment, was, in 1694, chief justice and vice-admiral.

Messrs. Copley, Blakiston, Jowles, Robothom, Greenbury and Addison, and Robert King, John Brooke and Robert Mason, esquires, judges of the provincial court, were commissioned by the crown, and afterwards were added, sir Thomas Lawrence and captain Nicholson. Edward Wynne, esquire, was appointed attorney-general, and Mr. Cheseldine, commissary-general.

Charles Carroll, Esq. succeeded colonel Darnall as chief agent of Lord Baltimore; though it appears that Edward Somersett, esquire, who had married Maria the daughter of Lord Baltimore, and died in the colony some years after, had a share in the agency as trustee of his father-in-law, part of the time that the government was held by the crown.

After passing an act of recognition, wherein they declared William and Mary to be sovereigns of England and *all its dominions*, and repealing all the former laws, except those which related to individual rights, governor Copley and the assembly in 1692 *prayed*, in the stile of British statutes, "that an act might be passed for establishing the Protestant religion." In pursuance of which, and with the assistance of doctor Thomas Bray, expressly commissioned for that purpose by the bishop of London, the colony was immediately divided into parishes, provided with vestry men and forty pounds of tobacco per poll, in lieu of tythes, levied for the support of the clergymen; of whom however, it is said, there were but sixteen in the first instance. Naturalization laws were superceded by a general act, declaring aliens who should take the oath of allegiance, fully naturalized. A duty was laid on spirits imported for the support of government, besides one shilling, or half the duty on tobacco exported. The colonists paid the new governor twenty-five pounds of tobacco per poll, annually, and a duty of three pence per hogshead on that article, and also appointed and supported an agent or attorney in England, independent of the proprietary.

In 1692, captain Francis Nicholson was appointed a councillor and held a commission of lieutenant-governor of Maryland and Virginia, but sir Edmund Andross, who had been governor of all the eastern colonies including New-York and the Jerseys, under James, and had so conducted himself as to be continued, was now governor-general of Virginia, had also a commission to succeed our governor and deputy in case of the death or absence of both. Governor Copley died in 1693, and captain Nicholson being in England, sir Edmond acted as governor of Virginia and Maryland until Mr. Nicholson's return, in 1694. In 1698 the latter succeeded to sir Edmond, as governor-general of Virginia and, after going to England, went to that colony. George Robothom, esquire, was appointed judge of vice-admiralty for the eastern-shore in 1694, and Henry Jowles, esquire, keeper of the great seal, and the year after, chancellor, keeper and judge of the court of vice-admiralty.

In the mean time, that is in 1694, under governor Nicholson, the *town land* at Proctor's on the Severn, with Oxford on the east side of the bay, were made ports of entry at which collectors or agents should reside. The former called Anne Arundel town, was the next year called Annapolis; the assembly holding its session there, making it the seat of justice of the county as well as the seat of the colonial government. Thus were the feelings of the Catholics of St. Mary's, by a removal from amongst them, saved from some of that mortification the revolution here was calculated to inflict, and of that odium in others in which their triumph might induce rivals to indulge.

The site of the capitol chosen by the Protestant government, was on good navigation, central and elevated, and the plan, consisting of two area's on which the state-house and church stands, with streets diverging from each, is convenient as well as elegant.

In a general system of education throughout the colony, adopted by the assembly on the recommendation of governor Nicholson, the foundation of the college was now began at the seat of government, by the appointment of trustees; and sundry imposts on the importation of negroes and spirits, and on skins, furs, beef and pork exported, except by inhabitants, or *English traders*, for the college and county and free schools, and for erecting court-houses, bridewells, &c. A duty was laid on officers, on spirits imported, ten pence on negroes and two shillings and six pence on white servants, and ten per cent on the amount of foreign goods exported, were also laid for the general expenses; then increased by the appropriation of three hundred and thirty-two pounds six shillings and eight pence, towards defraying the expenses of British forces employed on the frontiers of New-York against the French in Canada. The coast, especially from the south, being harrassed and plundered by daring pirates, punishments were provided for the offenders who might be taken and brought into the colony. It was thought necessary it seems, to have a surveyor-general of royal customs, to which office, Edward Randolph, esquire, was appointed; and it was now for the first time, that the governor and council, distinct from the upper-house and out of the assembly time, set as a court of appeals and writs of error; and appeals from thence in cases over three hundred pounds, were carried to the king and council in England. The gentlemen of the bar, for whose regulation many acts had been passed since the establishment of the province, were henceforth subjected to examinations before admittance, and judges and lawyers directed to wear gowns in court.

In 1695, Robert Smith, esquire, the chief justice, was appointed surveyor-general, and he had a deputy in each county, so that the office of register of the land office, was the only one held under the proprietary; and much difficulty he had, from the conflicting interests of the landlord in disposing of the lands; of which more than one half perhaps were yet vacant. Things in their nature inalienable, the soil and the sovereignty, being separated, it was perhaps impossible for persons of excellent intentions to avoid disputes in the position the officers were now placed. Warrants and surveys issued from the crown officers, on the terms fixed by Lord Baltimore, and his agents granted the patents, the records of which were claimed by the secretary of the colony, not of his appointment.

Prince George's county was laid off in this year by an act of assembly; from this Frederick county was taken in 1748; Queen Ann was erected in 1706; from which, and part of Dorchester county, Caroline was taken, and Harford from Baltimore in 1773; Worcester being taken from Somerset in 1742, all by different acts, made the sixteen counties existing at the commencement of the revolutionary war.

In 1696, the parliament of England passed an act declaring its laws to be paramount in the colonies; confined all trade to and from them, to British ships and property; and all sales of land therein, to *natural born* subjects only, and declared that all future proprietary governors should be approved of by the crown and take the oaths before they acted as such; and three years after, prohibited the exportation from them, of wool and woolen manufactures, and prescribed the punishment of piracy under condition of *forfeitures of charters.* In the same year, governor Nicholson, who had expelled the turbulent Mr. Coode from the colony, returned to England and was succeeded by Nathaniel Blaktston, esquire. Acts of assembly were passed permitting the Quakers to affirm; and to induce clergymen to remove to and settle in the colony, as expressly stated, prohibiting *magistrates* from celebrating marriages. The laws to encourage the importatation of negroes were revived, but others were passed restricting by heavy duties, the importation of *Irish Papists*, and that of flour was prohibited altogether.

The quit rents were farmed or leased in 1699, for seven years, to Messrs. Richard Bennet, and James Heath; a measure which was forced on Lord Baltimore, in all probability, by the difficulties opposed to his agents in the collection by the crown officers.

The population of Maryland, including eleven counties, at the commencement of the century, is stated by Holmes at twenty-five thousand; which it is supposed, was exclusive of the blacks, and perhaps of all other servants; although there were still Indian settlements at Piscataway. Of the number of one thousand, three hundred and fifty men, which the colonies from Carolina North, were to send against the Indians, who were excited and aided by the French from Canada and Louisianna, this colony was to furnish one hundred and sixty, by an act of assembly; and acts affording similar aid to the parent country, in men or money, were again passed in 1715, 1740, 1746, 1754, 1756, &c.

Queen Anne, who succeeded king William in 1702, adhered to his general colonial policy, and sent out colonel John Seymour to be governor of Maryland in 1704; during which interval it appears that the president of the council was Thomas

Tench, esq. The state-house erected at Annapolis was destroyed by fire, and many records of the province and of Anne Arundel county, 1704. Mr. Bacon states that some were lost by the removal from St. Mary's, and no doubt, many public documents were mislaid, if not entirely lost, by the removals from Annapolis when threatened with invasion, during the last and the preceeding war with England, so that our history will always be defective, it is to be apprehended.

After the passage of an act of recognition of the queen, the assembly enacted that none but natives or residents for three years, should hold offices, except those commissioned directly by the crown, and in an act entitled, "an act to prevent the growth of popery," Roman Catholic priests were prohibited from the public administration of worship. The acts of William and Mary in favour of dissenters, were enforced by laws passed here, and the affirmation of Quakers admitted in all cases accordingly. Parliament passed an act to establish the currency of the colonies at the rates before adopted here, and encourage the importation of naval stores from America. Lord Baltimore's right to dispose of the lands and receive his rents was not contested but the assembly again insisted that the queen should have the half of the two shillings tobacco duty, towards defraying expenses, which they repeated was no longer chargeable on the proprietary, and the government received it accordingly.

Then too, an act was passed limiting the interest of money debts at the then legal rate in England, that is, six per cent. per annum, that on products at eight per cent; and to prohibit the importation of bread, beer, flour, grain, horses, or tobacco, from Pennsylvania; but the necessities of the colonists, obliged them to prohibit the exportation and importation of such articles alternately; and, being generally planters or shippers, they actually prohibited all internal trade, by buying and selling under the name of *ingrossing*, which was probably the intention of former laws on the subject. Country bottoms or vessels were still exempted from certain new tonnage duties, and in 1706, hemp at six pence and flax at nine pence per pound, were made a legal tender for one fourth of all debts in money or tobacco, the latter valued at one penny per pound only.

Sir W. Davenant states the average quantity of tobacco imported into England for 1707, 1708 and 1709, at twenty-eight millions, eight hundred and fifty-eight thousand, six hundred and sixty-six pounds. At the same period, several acts of assembly were passed dividing the colony into commercial or maritime districts; that is, St. Mary's, St. George's and Annapolis were to be the chief places of three districts on the western-shore, and Chester, Oxford and Green Hill of as many on the eastern-shore, where naval officers should reside; and all vessels loading or unloading within either of them were to be under the inspection of the officer of such district; but it is stated that these acts were rejected by the crown. The city of St. Mary's lost its burgesses, when Annapolis obtained them by charter of queen Anne, in 1708.

At this time also the fees of the land office were limited by an act of assembly and surveyors required to take the oaths; both going to defeat the exercise of what little public authority might remain to the proprietary, or any preference he might have for people of his religious faith, but conformable no doubt to the laws of the parent country and indispensible of course. A law was passed for the relief of poor debtors, but suspended two years after, another was passed in 1724, but repealed the year after and never revived until 1774, but an act was passed and continued, to secure the payment of *country debts* from insolvent estates in *preference* to those of British or foreign origin; and one Richard Clarke, of Anne Arundel, was attainted and outlawed for treason and forgery.

In 1709, governor Seymour died and Edward Lloyd, esquire, was president of the council, and as such, the governor of the province.

In 1710, the British government established a general post-office in the colonies; the carriage of private letters being until then here, as it had been in England part of the preceeding century, altogether an object of individual enterprise; the transmission of the acts of the assembly were by the sheriffs fiom county to county, as were all other public dispatches. As before mentioned, the assembly granted three thousand acres of land to the Nanticoke Indians in Somerset county.

The chancellor and secretary, officers of the crown, continuing to exact fees on land affairs, Lord Baltimore renewed his instructions to Mr. Carroll in 1712, the latter being then in London, to require the same, as his agent, and as if none other were demanded, confirming all the proceedings of Mr. Darnall and that gentleman.

In 1714, John Hart, esquire, was appointed governor under the queen, and continued by her successor, and several acts passed calculated to relieve the inhabitants from the effects of the war just then terminated, though Maryland and the other middle colonies not then having European neighbors westward, suffered less than those on the north or south frontier. At this time the provincial court held exclusive jurisdiction in all cases real or mixt, in those of debts exceeding twenty pounds sterling, and in all criminal cases which were capital, except negroes, and so continued until 1773,

In 1715 an act of assembly was passed recognizing king George in the usual form, but he restored the province to the infant son of Benedict Leonard, who survived his father, the late lord Baltimore, only from the 21st February to the 16th of April, and had merely time to instruct the agent, Mr. Carroll, of his accession. A commission was sent out to Mr. Hart, by Charles, the new lord Baltimore, joined with lord Guilford his guardian; who exhibited a proof of his attention to the interest of the province, as well as of his ward, by a memorial presented to parliament against colonial regulations then proposed and in which was stated the amount of the proprietary's first expenditures, herein noticed already. Charles whose administration of the province as proprietary and as governor, was near 40 years, and was attended with so many difficulties but always honourable to himself, having married three times and living to the age of 85 years, has this best eulogium in the preamble of the act of 1674 renewing the port duty, which was past in consideration of the great favour of his lordship Cecilius, unto them, " in continuing his only son and heir apparent his governor," and gratefully acknowledged the *benefits they had received by his care and solicitude.* Charles had induced his son,

Benedict Leonard to renounce the Catholic religion, which he did a little before his father's decease and was elected member of parliament for Harwich directly after, so that the grandson and future heir, was educated in the established church, and thus was the legal impediment removed and the principal, if not the sole cause of the assumption of the government by the crown twenty seven years before.

It will be recollected that Benedict Leonard, now just deceased, was one of the infant governors of Maryland in the absence of his father. His lady was Charlotte, daughter of Edward Henry Lee, earl of Litchfield, and grand daughter of Charles the second, by the dutchess of Cleveland.

It was at this period, that is, after the accession of George the first and before the restoration of the province to Charles, the fifth Lord Baltimore, that the assembly under governor Hart passed those important laws still in force, in whole or in part, viz. to limit the damage on bills of exchange returned protested, at fifteen per cent. The power to bring actions on common debts or accounts at three years and on bonds, or other specialties at twelve years, with savings to infants, absentees, &c. commonly called the acts of limitation ; the acts directing the manner of sueing out attachments, and permitting the testimony of negroes in cases of other people of colour: they also extended the jurisdiction of the county courts in actions for debt where the balance did not exceed twenty pounds sterling, from which there should be no appeal under six pounds sterling, increasing the jurisdiction of single justices from sixteen shillings and eight pence to thirty three shillings and four pence.

There was no immediate change in the council except the appointment of Thomas Smith, Esq. The judges of the provincial court were William Holland, Esq. chief justice, Thomas Smyth, Samuel Young, Thomas Addison, Richard Tilghman, James Harris and Joseph Stoddert, esquires, associates. Messrs. Thos. Beake and Charles Lowe were secretaries, but the duties were performed by Philemon Lloyd, esq. deputy. Thomas Bordley, Esq. was attorney general and Mr. Carroll continued chief agent. No officers were commissioned or appointed by the government of England afterwards, except those to collect the

English duties or customs; and all fines and forfeitures, which had gone latterly to the crown, were restored to the proprietary for the future. The assemblies again divided into upper and lower houses, as they had been before established, but to vote for delegates or representatives, as they were now expressly called according to the charter, it was made requisite to possess a freehold of fifty acres of land, or an estate of forty pounds sterling at least; for though a quit rent was paid, the tenure was always considered fee simple or freehold, as before observed.

Voters were subjected to fines if they neglected to attend the polls, which were to be held by the sheriffs before some of the justices, as often as the governor should issue writs for the purpose, and a daily allowance was provided for the assemblymen, of whom there were to be four for each county and two for a city or borough, and not to be *ordinary keepers* or such others as were excluded from the British parliament. The sheriffs were excluded, being specially judges of the elections, but the returns were to be made under the hands and seals of all the *electors*, as well as of the sheriffs.

A general revision of the laws took place. Those relating to religion were confirmed, with an oath of abjuration, in imitation of that adopted in England against the pretender. Widows or stepfathers who were Roman catholics were not allowed to educate the children of protestant fathers; but the courts were bound to enquire by special juries, whether orphans were provided agreeably to their estates, and, such as were apprentices, taught their trades and not put to common labour. A union of offices in some instances, and a reduction of them in others, under the proprietary, lessened the burthens and facilitated the transaction of business, and the differences between his agents and the governor, relative to the revenue and land office, subsided on the resignation of the latter four years after. Lord Baltimore received the tonnage & half of the duty on tobacco exported, as formerly; duties were added on spirits, negroes & servants imported, and an assessment for public expenses besides, but the assembly itself ventured to leave the *small provincial charges* to be levied by the governor and council during the intervals of its sessions, which were sometimes over the year.

The council still forming the upper house and court of appeals, was generally composed of the high officers in the province, and though it rendered that body more subservient to his views, than hereditary, or elected and independent senators would have been, it was the interest of the proprietary to use his influence to shield the colonists from the exactions of the British government, and against the pretensions of the proprietary himself, appeals were made to the crown.——The proprietary governments, except indeed where they were vested in a number of individuals or commercial companies, were therefore, more popular than the royal, although the latter received some succours from the crown at an early period, which the former did not; as in Bacon's rebellion in Virginia, and in defending New England against their French and Dutch neighbours; and the form now restored in Maryland was preserved until independence was declared; which, including the periods of revolutions noticed was 120 years, or nearly from the foundation of the settlement to that period.

Although premiums were still given for killing bears and wolves, wild horses and cattle were so numerous that it became a business to pursue them, which proves that the settlements were remote and *Rangers* were licensed by law, that being the name of frontier guards, and others were passed to preserve the Deer, with some exceptions in favour of Indians, of whom there were settlements on the Monococy still.

A more full and energetic militia system was adopted with their rates of pay while in active service. Press masters, appointed by court, if directed by the governor or commandant, were authorized to take stores in each county for the use of the military on service.

The councillors were generally colonels of militia, and we find soon after, that two of them, Messrs. Matthew Tilghman Ward and Levin Gale were appointed major generals.

In 1718 Roman Catholics were expressly prohibited from voting unless they took the oath of allegiance and abjuration, but the acts of assembly to prevent the *growth of popery*, passed during the late reigns, were repealed, refering to the existing acts of parliament, as paramount and sufficient for the purposes intended. Mr. Carroll and others, of the Roman Catholic faith, continuing to hold their offices notwithstanding the late change, the proprietary's agents in land affairs were expressly exempted from any disqualification on account of religion. Anxious to direct the colonists from manufactures, the government of England granted bounties on the importation of iron, and the legislature passed an act in 1719 to lay off a hundred acres of land by appraisement to those who would set up furnaces and forges, similar to the grants which had been made for mills. Much ore being found, several Iron works were erected on the western shore, and great quantities of wood land taken up by the owners.

In 1720 Charles Calvert, esquire, a relation of the proprietary, superceeded Mr. Hart as governor, and all the difficulties of the land office ceased, but it is probable that Mr. Calvert, like succeeding governors, were approved by the crown after being nominated by the proprietary, and which though it produced no contentions that we learn and however moderately exercised, was no less a violation of his charter.

In 1721 executions on all judgments whatever, were suspended from May to November, and afterwards until February, as those of the county courts had been for many years before, in order that the labours of the field might not be interrupted: Soon after, the workmen at furnaces, forges and mills were exempted from work on the highways, which at that time were repaired, by the labour of all male taxables, and the taxables were declared by the acts of 1715 and 1725, to include all males, and all coloured women, aged sixteen and upwards, but clergymen, paupers and incapacitated negroes were excepted.

In 1723 courts of assize, composed of two provincial court justices for each shore, were organized and continued to exercise some powers superior to the county courts in all the counties until about twenty years after.

The funds provided for schools being now sufficient, visitors were appointed for every county; and such children as they directed to be taught gratis were to be received in these schools, under penalty of dismissal of teachers, who could be protestants only, but no persons children were exempt on account of religion ; not but there had been some progress in these establishments before, especially at Oxford, which was a capital for the eastern shore sometime. Peltry and copper ore were added by parliament to the articles which must go direct to England, and seven years after naval stores, staves and boards were added.

In 1727 Benedict Leonard Calvert, esquire, brother of the proprietary, F. R. S. and member of parliament for Harwich, was appointed governor and came out to Maryland, but taking ill embarked for England in 1732 and died on the passage, having appointed Samuel Ogle, esquire, governor in his place the year before.

In 1728 Edward Henry, another brother of the proprietary, was appointed commissary general and president of council. Persons importing convicts were compelled to enter them as such, and declare the crimes of which they had been convicted, as well for the security of the inhabitants as to enforce the duty imposed on such importations.

In 1729 a premium of fifteen per cent. was allowed on duties paid in specie imported, and the inhabitants of Baltimore county petitioned for and obtained the laying out of the town of the same name on sixty acres of Mr Carroll's land, which he was paid for at 40 shillings per acre, and it was first represented in 1774, but not incorporated until twenty years after. Chester in Kent, was laid out by act of 1706, but Easton not until after independence, as were Elkton, Hagerstown and Cumberland. Where towns were on the proprietary's lands, he received one cent per lot or acre per annum quit rent.

In M'Phersons annals it is stated, that in 1731, the tobacco imported into Great Britain from Virginia and Maryland, amounted to sixty thousand hogsheads, lumber to the value of fifteen thousand pounds, and skins and furs about six thousand pounds sterling; employing twenty four thousand tons of shipping; at this time it is also stated that the two provinces raised about the same quantity of tobacco each. This staple was however so reduced in price the ensuing year in Maryland, that a number of fields of plants were destroyed by the malcontents; and the militia were called out to suppress them and punishments provided by law for the offenders.

In 1732 Lord Baltimore and John, Thomas, and Richard

Penn, esquires, the surviving sons of William Penn, entered into an agreement to settle their limits by arbitration, taking for the basis the bounds of the territory conquered from the Dutch, as ceded to Mr. Penn, and from those bounds north, until within fifteen miles of the latitude of Philadelphia, and from that parrallel due west, across the Susquehanna river, &c. Seven arbitrators were appointed by each party three of whom to have power to act; on his part Lord Baltimore appointed Samuel Ogle, esquire the governor, and Messrs. Charles Calvert, Philemon Lloyd, Michael Howard, Richard Bennet, Benjamin Tasker, and Matthew Tilghman Ward commissioners, and came out himself; Mr. Thomas Penn also coming to Pennsylvania. A meeting took place at Newcastle, but differences occurring in relation to the situation of the cape, or point, at which the Dutch territory on Delaware began, and the manner of describing the periphery at New Castle, the arbitrators seperated, and the parties again returned to England. So far as concerned the division line of the peninsula, it had been determined by the lords of trade as early as 1685 and could but be satisfactory to Lord Baltimore, as he was compelled to yield the Delaware shore; for a ridge where the waters run into each bay in opposite directions, carrying with them the interests of the respective inhabitants, *and* which was not likely to become a highway for nations, would most probably secure future peace; but the cape called Henlopen, being twenty miles south of Delaware bay, would, if fixed as a beginning, deprive our proprietary of several thousand square miles of land well timbered, which he could not willingly assent to loose. Both parties intended originally no doubt, the entrance of the bay called cape *Cornelius*, then *James*, for a beginning, but that was called *Inlopen* and the outer cape *Henlopen*, in the old Dutch charts; the former had lost its original appellation before this agreement was entered into, but the latter remained and was referred to in that instrument, by mistake, as it is supposed. To remedy this, and get himself justice, Lord Baltimore endeavoured to procure a new grant from the crown, but was refused. Mr. Penn's heirs filed a bill in chancery, and in 1750, obtained a decree of lord Hardwicke confirming the agreement and bounds proposed on their part according to the name of the outer cape in the old charts.

The improvements in English manufactures, the credit given there and the necessity of using it here, the low price of the staple and the scarcity of specie notwithstanding the bounty lately offered on its importation, much more going to the other colonies, where there was already a depreciated paper calculated to invite speculation at the expense of their neighbours, the example was now followed by Maryland. A bill for thirty six thousand pounds had been passed two years before, but not sanctioned by the proprietary. Witnessing himself the distresses of the province afterwards, ninety thousand pounds were created in 1733, redeemable in 31 years by a duty of one shilling & three pence per hhd. on tobacco payable in bills of exchange, to be remitted and invested in British bank stock by three commissioners, under the direction of the proprietary who was to appoint them. A portion of those bills of credit was to be paid to planters at thirty shillings per taxable person, for the burning of three hundred pounds of *trash* tobacco; and they were receivable in taxes in lieu of that article, at the same rate of ten shillings per hundred pounds, & a legal tender of all future contracts for money, the dues of the church and proprietary only excepted.—A thousand pounds currency were granted each county for public buildings, and three thousand pounds appropriated for a government house; the remainder was to be loaned for limited times, on mortgage or personal security, at four per cent. interest, being two per cent. less than the rate established. It was in fact, a banking system, which, properly managed, would not only relieve individuals and accelerate improvements, but, as far as the demands of circulation required, would supercede the ordinary taxes. Loans were repeated and new emissions authorised, thirty four thousand and fifteen pounds six shillings during the Canada war for instance, until they became a substitute for all other money and fell, but the result will be seen hereafter, when *pay day* came round. It is stated in Mr. Douglass's summary, that in 1748, one hundred pounds sterling sold for two hundred pounds of our currency of six shillings to the dollar at which rate it is also stated in the gentleman's magazine for 1755, but the exchange was *five* times as high in several colonies both eastward and southward, where in consequence thereof, the British government interfered to prevent excessive issues by them.

Before his departure from England Lord Baltimore had been elected a member of the royal society and appointed gentleman of the bed chamber to prince Frederick, grandfather to the present king; on his return he was appointed one of the lords of the admiralty and elected member of parliament for Surry and of the society for propagating the gospel.

At this period the proprietary required forty shillings sterling per hundred acres as caution or consideration, besides the yearly rent of land, and this was raised to above four shillings per annum and sometimes ten shillings, according to quality and situation, at the discretion in some measure of his agents, but, additions by re-surveys, to be at original prices or valuation of the surveyors in cases of escheat, and alienations by devise were expressly exempted from the fine. Mr. Ogle became governor again on the departure of the proprietary in 1734.

It is stated in the Universal History that Maryland employed one hundred and thirty sail of ships in 1736, and that from this province and Virginia, there was exported the value of two hundred and ten thousand pounds sterling, which no doubt had been greater if the trade was not still restricted to British dominions and the south of Europe. The number of vessels of this province is stated at two hundred in the Gent. Magazine, and at the same period and afterwards laws were passed to refund several persons the duties which had been paid on tobacco lost at sea.

In 1737 the exportation of grain, bread and flour was prohibited for a year, and in 1740, the hard winter, a considerable sum was appropriated for the enlistment of troops for the king's service against the Spanish West Indies, and in 1746 this province raised three hundred men to join the other forces against the French and Indians from Canada. In the same year 1737, James Harris esquire, was appointed surveyor general of the eastern shore, and there were seperate surveyor generals for each shore afterwards.

The winter of 1740 is said to have been excessively cold, and not surpassed since, except by that of 1779 and 1783, in both which Chesapeake bay was closed by ice to the mouth of Patowmack.

The ice which began to make on the first of January 1784 did not open at Patuxent until the ninth of March, at Patapsco until the sixteenth nor at Baltimore until the twenty-fifth, which was sixteen days later than 1780. In the Philosophical Transactions for 1759 it is stated that the mercury in Fahrenheit's Thermometer in the year 1753 ranged in *Maryland* from ten degrees the lowest to ninety degrees the greatest heat, the mean being sixty degrees, but from observations made near Baltimore by Lewis Brantz, esquire, for several years just past, the range is from ten below Zero to ninety eight and the mean temperature about fifty two, which is the temperature of the spring water in this city. Thus it appears that the popular opinion relating to the improved temperature is not founded in fact, and so doctor Rush expressly stated in his latter publications. But all agree that with us, the north west winds are most prevalent and that they are accompanied by clear wholesome weather. The fall of water on an average of the years 1817 to 1820 inclusive, by the notes of Mr. Brantz, was thirty eight inches. We are visited occasionally by severe thunder and lightning; earthquakes or hurricanes are scarcely felt or known in Maryland, but the climate is so variable that vegetation commences sometimes early in March, at others not until the beginning of May; the small grain is got in generally early in July, and the fall of the leaf is from the first of October to the middle of November.

Thomas Bladen, esquire, having gone to England, married miss Jansen, an elder sister of lady Baltimore and returned governor in 1742. In 1744 by treaty with Indians at Lancaster, at which Maryland was represented by Edmund Jennings, Philip Thomas, Robert King and Thomas Colvill, esquires, the western bounds of the province were settled by a line from the head of the North branch of Patowmack, north to the Pennsylvania line; no other line being settled it is the present division between Virginia and Maryland, and gives to the former more lands than if the same bounds had run from the head of the south branch of that river. But at that time both colonies gained by reducing their western frontier and it is believed the British board of trade determined the line as so run, the year after. It was however the former year that the assembly created a town on Indian river calling it *Baltimore*, but within Mr. Penn's claim, and proves that the sense of the province was with the proprietary of Maryland at the time.

By the provisions of an act relating to Charles town in Cecil county, laid out two years before, appointing an inspector, it appears that the manufacture and trade of flour began to attract the attention of the government at this time. It is probable that the vicinity of this place to the fertile grain counties of Chester and Lancaster in Pennsylvania, had created a market for wheat and flour at Charles town before those articles had been produced in any considerable quantities to the south, although they have now succeeded to be staple articles of Maryland, in as great if not greater extent than tobacco now is or perhaps ever was; and a few years after this period provision was also made for regulating the trade in flour at Baltimore and Georgetown. Such a change was anticipated and announced to the American Philosophical Society by doctor Williamson in 1770, from an amelioration of the climate by cultivation, but we apprehend it is sufficiently accounted for by the scarcity of new grounds for tobacco in proportion to the increased culture, & the want of proper husbandry to preserve or improve tobacco grounds on the one hand, and on the other, the usual advantages derived from a change of crops and the high prices obtained for flour during the latter times. The regulation alluded to consisted chiefly in declaring that no flour should be exported until inspected and branded for good and merchantable. About this time also the inspection of tobacco was put on nearly the same footing in which it now is. The fees of the inspectors had been converted to fixed salaries, as the only means to prevent corruption in such offices where there was a concurrence; and the inspectors, which then and for a long time before, had been nominated by the parish vestries, are since the revolution presented by the Levy courts of the counties. Though tobacco was always sold by the hundred pounds, as long as flour was sold by weight which it was until after independence, the hundred weight consisted of one hundred and twelve pounds and the exportation of wheat; which was considerable before that event, ceased soon after, in consequence of the improvements in mills and the manufacture of flour.

In 1745 Mr. Jonas Green, who had been five years printer of the laws, commenced the paper called the *Maryland Gazette,* which he published weekly at Annapolis. It is continued by one of his descendants, twice a week, and it may be asserted without hazard, is the oldest establishment of the kind in North America.

Governor Bladen began the house for which funds had been long provided and intended for the residence of such officers, but not being finished it was used by the college; that gentleman returning to England in 1746 Samuel Ogle, esquire, was appointed governor for the third time.

In 1748 Frederick county was taken off from Prince George's and then included all the lands of Montgomery, Washington and Allegheny counties westward, there being already a town then called Frederick. The tobacco trade at this time was said to employ twenty five thousand seamen and yield to Great Britain, by exports at the duty of six pence per pound, one million a year, besides the consumption of seven millions pounds there.

In 1750, some further encouragement was given to the making of iron, but slitting mills and tilt hammers were prohibited in the colonies by act of parliament. The next year Georgetown on Patowmack was laid out on like terms with other towns.

Frederick only surviving son of Lord Baltimore became proprietary while a minor, by the death of his father the twenty third April 1751, aged fifty two years. Having already noticed several particulars in the private life of Charles the fifth Lord Baltimore, it may only be added here, that he married Mary daughter of sir Theodore Jansen of Wimbledon in Surry; that he devised the reversion of the province to his daughters and their male heirs, in succession, in case of default of such heirs to his son, and appointed Messrs. Bladen and Ogle two of the executors; that in the Chronicles of the time, he is represented as a man of elegant person and address, learned himself and a patron of science, enjoying a splendid revenue in a princely style, and that the parsimony of George the second, who confided to him the chief offices about his son, put it in his power to render such munificent services to the prince who died the same year, as would probably have secured to him the highest honors in the state had they survived the king.

In 1752 the British parliament altered the calender, by which the new year commenced the first of January instead of the 25th of March, and the dates used in these sketches from the beginning, as far as could be ascertained, are according to the *new style.* Governor Ogle going to England, Benjamin Tasker, esquire, was president and as such governor of the colony until Horatio Sharpe, esquire, was appointed governor in 1753. According to the Annual Register, the imports into England this year from Virginia and Maryland, amounted to six hundred and thirty two thousand five hundred and seventy four pounds four shillings and eight pence, and the exports to three hundred and fifty six thousand seven hundred and seventy six pounds eleven shillings and three pence, making a balance of two hundred and seventy five thousand seven hundred and ninety seven pounds thirteen shillings and five pence in favour of the provinces. The white population is stated by other authorities to be about seventy thousand each, but soon after a very particular census of Maryland was published in the Gentleman's Magazine, by which it appears there were then in the province:

	Free.	*Servants.*	*Convicts.*	*Total.*
Men,	24058	3576	1507	29141
Women,	23521	1824	386	25731
Boys,	26637	1049	67	27752
Girls,	24141	422	21	24584
	98357	6870	1981	107,208

By the same account the number of mulattoes amounted to	3,592
And that of Negroes to - - - -	42,764
Total,	153,564*

* A general census of all the colonies was taken by direction of Congress in 1776, but the result is unknown to us.

In anticipation of another war with the French, who now held forts and instigated the Indians on the westward from the lakes to the Mississippi, a congress of the provincial and colonial governments was held at Albany in 1754, to which Benjamin Tasker and Charles Carroll junior esquires were sent by Maryland, for the purpose of treating with the Six Nations: and at which articles of confederation were drawn up by a committee of which Mr. Tasker was one, for the approbation of the parliament and colonial assemblies, but was rejected by each as too favorable to the other. It appears that no delegates were present from the royal government of Virginia or the other colonies south, and that a submission of all the colonial governments to the controul of a governor general of royal appointment, was the object of the crown and not likely to be assented to here. It was in the same year, general then colonel Washington, had gone to the neighbourhood of the Ohio with Virginia troops, and first conquered and then was obliged to surrender fort Necessity. Maryland provided for the erection of forts and blockhouses towards the frontiers, sent Messrs. Tasker and Carroll to procure Indian alliances, and placed a number of troops under the command of the Maryland lieutenant colonel Dagworthy, commanding at Cumberland, a new fort on the Patowmack, beyond the colony's fort *Frederick*, which last was near Hancock town and erected sometime before. Our colonel then a British captain only Judge Marshall says, claiming to rank above colo-

In 1790, our population was, -	White	208,647
	Slaves	103,036
	Coloured	8,043
Total		319,726
In 1820, the population was, -	White	260,222
	Slaves	107,398
	Coloured	39,730
Total		407,350

Males 206,862—females 200,488. Excess of males 6,374.

The following statement published since the last census in 1820, is inserted here to show the present number in each coun-

nel Washington the latter refused to pass the Patowmack. An act of assembly was passed "for taking and detaining able bodied men," and a supply of forty thousand pounds was granted for the service, under Dagworthy and afterwards under general Forbes. To defray the expences of which armament the assembly increased the former duties, and laid taxes, viz. one shilling per hundred acres on land, the proprietary's manors not exempt, on horses forty shillings, carriages of pleasure five shillings per wheel, billiard tables sixty shillings, pedlars eighty shillings and on batchelors five shillings. Judiciary proceedings and conveyances were also taxed, and the lands of the Catholic's were assessed double; ten pounds and afterwards fifty pounds were to be paid for each Indian prisoner or *scalp, being the skin of the crown of the head,* to any person except *Soldiers* or Indian *allies,* being that kind of indemnity to which savages were accustomed and most likely to tempt enemies to become friends. Some of them were subsidised by the colony and a party of Cherokees visiting the seat of government as allies,

---

ty with the increase or decrease in ten years, to which is added the date of the erection of the respective counties.

	Number 1810.	*Number* 1820.	*Increase.*	*Decrease.*	*Erected*
St. Mary's	12794	12974	180		1634
Kent	11450	11453	3		1634
Anne Arundel	26668	27165	497		1650
Calvert	8005	8073	68		1654
Charles	20245	16500		3745	1658
Baltimore	29255	33463	4208		1659
Talbot	14230	14389	159		1661
Somerset	17195	19579	2384		1666
Dorchester	18108	17759		349	1669
Cecil	13066	16048	2982		1674
Prince George's	20589	20216		373	1695
Queen Anne's	16648	14952		1696	1706
Worcester	16971	17421	450		1742
Frederick	34437	40459	6022		1748
Harford	18275	15924		2351	1773
Caroline	9453	10108	655		1773
Washington	18730	23075	4345		1776
Montgomery	17980	16400		1580	1776
Allegheny	6909	8654	1745		1789
Baltimore city	46555	62738	16183		1729

received a considerable sum of money, and the most friendly treatment.

From a dispute between the two branches of the legislature, the upper house rejected some of the bills of supplies, and the province was charged with a refusal to sustain its part of the expense of this war; but very unjustly, as was stated by doctor Franklin to the parliament; nor can there be any doubt on the subject, when it is recollected that the savages passed our forts on the Patowmack and spread terror amongst the inhabitants of the oldest counties on the western shore, and to the bay side, after the defeat of general Braddock. They were met and routed at St. George's creek and Loyal Hanning in 1758, but attacked colonel Thomas Cressap's house, when they were also defeated in 1762, a few captives being taken out of their hands and about three hundred pounds being paid for *scalps* at the different engagements, agreeably to the law.

In 1758 sir William Johnstone, appointed Indian agent by the government of England, with some of the governors, concluded a treaty with the Six Nations and some other Indi ns, among whom there were Nanticokes who had voluntarily gone from Maryland. But this treaty had been preceeded by the evacuation by the French and Indians of fort *Duquesne*, now named fort Pitt, in honor of the minister just appointed, and whose councils had produced a turn of affairs so favourable as to endear him to the colonists. The war terminated in 1763, three years after the accession of George the third, by the expulsion of the French and Spanish from all their colonies on this continent north of the gulf of Mexico and Mississippi. The colonists had contributed essentialiy to these acquisitions, in which as frontiers they were so much interested; for instigating of the Indians by the French and Spanish, which did not cease even with the public hostilities, had created such violent animosities against those nations, in colonies exposed to savage vengeance, that they entered into the contest with vigour; indeed the very religion those European enemies professed became more obnoxious, and its professors suffered some persecutions besides those already noticed. The inhabitants seem to have forgotten that liberality in which the province was founded, and which, as early as 1676, had fostered the Protestants and produced the establishment of many Episcopal and other churches, to recall the intolerant spirit of acts passed during the unsettled state of the parent country and generously repealed by their predecessors on the restoration of the province to Lord Baltimore. Of these dispositions the British government which had voted some money to reimburse the colonies, and passed some acts to encourage the importation of staves and heading from them, thought to avail itself in 1664, laying new duties on sugar, coffee, wine, silks, cambrics, &c. and in 1765, the colonies were subjected to stamps upon papers, legal and mercantile. But now a congress was assembled for very different purposes than the last; and William Murdock, Edward Tilghman and Thomas Ringgold, esquires, deputies, went from Maryland to the above congress at New York; when it was declared on the part of all the colonies north of the Patowmack, that the colonists had the exclusive right to tax themselves, and the British government was addressed accordingly. Mr. Zachariah Hood, to whom the stamps were sent for this province, was forced to quit Annapolis, and in fact resigned. No stamps were distributed or paid for in these colonies, but non-importation agreements were entered into generally throughout the continent. An act was passed the next year by the assembly of Maryland, to regulate the entry of vessels with passengers infected by contagious maladies. The Stamp act was repealed in 1766; but, in pursuance of the authority to which they considered themselves entitled, the parliament immediately asserted their power to tax the colonists in all cases whatever.

Messrs. Charles Mason and Jeremiah Dixon, astronomers of celebrity in England, chosen and sent out by the respective proprietaries for the purpose, completed the division lines between the provinces of Pennsylvania and Maryland.

The form of the latter, of which a very good map was made and published by Dennis Griffith, esquire, in 1794, situated between thirty eight and thirty nine degrees forty minutes north latitude, and one degree fifty eight east and two degrees twenty four west longitude from Washington; resembling an irregular angle, of which the base is the north bound, or east and west line, two hundred miles long, terminating at the former by a line nearly north and south, of about eighty seven miles, but which then runs eastwardly about thirty five miles to the sea, and binding on that about forty five miles to the line of Virginia, then with that line, and the river Patowmack to its head or source, and thence by a short line due north to the first mentioned line or base. Maryland is supposed to contain a superfice of seven million acres, of which one and a half million acres are in water. Every part of it is within thirty miles of boatable navigation, and, exclusive of that, the quantities of fish render the water almost as valuable as the land. The Granite ridge, which commences in New England and runs by the head of the inlets at the west side of the bay, to the southern states, divides this into two nearly equal parts, so that one half the soil may be considered original and the other alluvial: but the colonists found all a forest.*

In 1766, and in consequence as it is stated in Hanson's laws, "of the scarcity of specie & public credit being reduced to an extreme low condition in consequence of a difference which had long subsisted between the two houses respecting the claim of the clerk of the upper house, and which had for several years prevented the passage of the journal or of the taking any measures for discharging the public debts" & although there was due the province twenty-one thousand and eighty-eight pounds two shillings and six pence sterling of tobacco debt at seven shillings & six pence per hundred pounds, & the sum of nineteen

* Doctor Morse having stated the quantity of lands in the state at fourteen thousand square miles and Dr. Seybert estimates the population in 1810, at 27-13 per square mile and 1-19th of the population of the union, 95-63 females for every hundred males, 45-16 slaves for every hundred free persons; that the returns of the militia were thirty-three thousand four hundred and ten, and that in respect to square miles, Maryland ranked the eleventh; in population the eighth; in federal representation the seventh; domestic exports the sixth; manufactures the fifth; and in the totals of exports, tonnage or revenue the fourth state,

thousand eight hundred & forty-one pounds one shilling and two pence *nominal* money, equal at the real exchange, to eleven thousand nine hundred & four pounds twelve shillings & eight pence sterling, together thirty-two thousand nine hundred & ninety-two pounds fifteen shillings and two pence sterling, besides twenty six thousand eight hundred pounds bank stock and five thousand two hundred and thirty pounds seventeen shillings and two pence interest not invested; an emission of bills of credit was ordered to the amount of one hundred and seventy-three thousand seven hundred and thirty three dollars to pay the debts. The bills were to be redeemed in 1777 by drafts on the trustees in London, which happening during the revolution, drafts on them were refused payment and was not effected of course. Three years after another emission of three hundred and eighteen thousand dollars was ordered, for the purpose of lending on interest to the inhabitants at four per cent. per annum redeemable by the money of the preceeding creation or by bills on London; though bills were to be drawn instead of issues when exchange was above par, and the whole was to be taken out of circulation in twelve years, which brought it under the predicament of the other; that is to say, to be sunk by depreciation, lost to individuals when received by them for money and the bank stock remained for the treasury.

The investments in London, which in 1776, by the fidelity of the commissioners both at Annapolis and there, amounted to thirty thousand pounds sterling, survived the shock; and from a spirit of commercial justice in that government, elicited by the talents of Messrs. Chase, P in ey and other agents, six hundred and fifty thousand dollars were received in 1805, even after a large discount to the proprietary and others in England.

In 1767, after some favorable changes in the customs, relating to the transit and duties on West India produce in the colonies, parliament laid duties on the importation here of tea, glass, paper and colours from England. These were resisted as the stamps had been, and more violently, for a cargo which had arrived at Annapolis was thrown into the river, the consignees being themselves compelled by the inhabitants to effect it. All the teas were either burned, destroyed or returned from every port to which they were sent, although it was declared the proceeds were to be spent in defence of the colonies, and salted provision and raw hides were to be admitted in England from them free of duties.

In 1768 a law was passed providing for the erection of alms and work houses and trustees of the poor in several counties; which by other laws has since been extended to all; the poor being, previously, supplied at their own houses by county levies annually.

Lord Baltimore had the misfortune to loose his lady, who was Diana, daughter of Scrope Egerton, duke of Bridgewater, by the overturning of a carriage in 1758, and not marrying again, led a dissolute life. He was this year prosecuted for an offence highly criminal, but voluntarily submitted to his trial in the court of King's bench setting at Kingston in Surry, where his country residence was, and where he asserted his innocence before a jury of the county with eloquence and success.

The Nanticoke Indians represented that they were few remaining and were desirous to dispose of their lands, provision was made by law for that purpose; and thirty years after, the Choptank Indians made a similar representation with the same effect, but a few of the descendants of these Indians are still, or were lately, remaining in that neighborhood under the pay and protection of the state government.

From general Wilkinson's memoirs we learn that about this time, doctor Henry Stevenson of Baltimore, introduced the practice of inoculation with more celebrity, at least, in this part of the country by receiving patients into his spacious new house there; which practice was succeeded by vaccination thirty years after, very much by the zeal of doctor James Smith of the same place being aided by the state soon after.

In the same year Robert Eden, esquire, who had married Caroline, the youngest daughter of the late Lord Baltimore, was appointed governor and arrived in Maryland.

In 1769, Mr. William Rumsey of this province, with other members of the American Philosophical Society, took the levels and made estimates for a canal between the Chesapeake and Delaware, and thirty-five thousand dollars of bills of credit were authorised for erecting the present splendid state house at Annapolis, which was not completed before the revolution.

Messrs. Daniel Dulany, Thomas Johnson, John Hall, William Paca, Charles Carroll, Barrister, Lancelot Jacques and Charles Wallace were appointed commissioners to superintend the erection of the state-house, on a spacious eminence for the improvement of which, 500 pounds sterling were appropriated, out of the bills just created. Mr. William Anderson was the architect, but it received its present finish several years after by Mr. Joseph Clarke. It is chiefly built of brick made at Annapolis. Its front to the south-east, is one hundred and thirty feet and the depth one hundred feet, divided into six rooms on each of two floors, besides a spacious vestibule, court-room and an area, about forty feet square, over which the dome, of the same diameter, is raised to the height of one hundred and eleven feet. After raising a few steps to the portico which is fifteen feet wide, the height from the platform to the cornish is thirty-six feet, and the dome, galery, acorn and spire makes the whole about two hundred feet. From the galery there is a delightful view of the city and harbor of Annapolis, the country round and Severn and South rivers, besides a distant and interesting prospect of the bay and eastern-shore.

It was remarked in England, that the Americans who used to take at least eighth of the State Lottery tickets, had nearly suspended all such adventures. As no lotteries had then been authorised by our laws, this at least was one effect of colonial retaliation.

According to the Encyclopedia Britannica there were entered in Maryland in 1770, two hundred and five ships, and one hundred and ninety-seven sloops, and cleared two hundred and twenty-eight ships and one hundred and seventy-two sloops; and the amount of exports the year before, was *one million, five hundred and fifty-four thousand, four hundred and thirty dollars* at four shillings and six-pence sterling per dollar. Governor Eden bought and improved the house at Annapolis used at present by the governors, being confiscated during the revolution.

Frederick the 6th and last Lord Baltimore dying in 1771, in Italy, aged forty years, without legitimate children, the title of Baron of Baltimore became extinct, but Henry Harford, esq. a natural son, was declared proprietary, though a minor, in virtue of his father's will; of which Messrs, Eden, Hammersly, Provost and Morris were executors, and by which Lord Baltimore gave a reversion to Mrs. Windham, Mr. Harford's sister, who was first clandestinely married to Mr. Morris and divorced; then to his own younger sister Caroline, Mrs. Eden, with a legacy of *twenty thousand* pounds between her and his oldest sister Louisa, then Mrs. Browning, if they assented to the will.

Whatever was the aberance of the last Lord Baltimore, he did not participate in the late offensive measures. Maryland continued to grow in people, wealth and happiness under his proprietaryship. Men of genius and enterprise were found in every county, and the capital had become a little court of taste and fashion. If the tree which was so fairly planted by Cecilius, and so faithfully nurtured by the first and second Charles, yielded a fruit of which the exuberance intoxicated their successor, the stock increased, spreading its branches majestically, and the excrecences being lopped off in later times, it remains an heir-loom, of which they who claim it by adoption as well as those who hold it from birthright, may well be proud.

The exports to and imports from Great Britain in 1773 were greater than they had been twenty years before, because these colonies increased in wealth by the more extensive trade with the interior and other colonies lately acquired: As the importations from England must have been materially affected by public and private associations to use domestic goods. Much of this trade was no doubt forced, on British account, especially that of imports here, in anticipation of a total loss of the market.

Provision was made by the legislatures of Maryland and Virginia for erecting a light-house on Cape Henry, by a duty of four pence per ton on vessels entering either colony. The jurisdiction of the county courts was now extended in criminal cases and matters of debt, to be concurrent with that of the provincial court. A concurrent jurisdiction with the Chancellor in cases in equity not exceeding twenty pounds, had been given the county courts in 1763; the jurisdiction of single justices was now extended to fifty shillings, or eight dollars and thirty-three and a third cents, without fees; and the tobacco fees were regulated at rates which, when reduced to money at one dollar sixty-six and two-thirds per cent, were exceedingly low, as they have been always and continue in Maryland, as well as the salaries of all offices. It appears that delegates to the assembly received a compensation in proportion to their expences from early times, and justices of the peace and jurors also, whilst attending court.

The limitation of jurisdiction to the provincial court in all criminal cases which were capital, except committed by negroes until now; would have been an intolerable grievance to the counties, if the perpetration of such crimes had been frequent. The same cause as to civil affairs, the charge of attending the high court at the seat of government, in all important cases, must have prohibited the people from a baneful spirit of litigation. To have been so much exempted from contests among one another, from murders and felonies destructive to life and morals, wasno doubt a source of great happiness; and to be relieved from the pain of witnessing executions or other capital punishments, in great measure, could scarcely be less condusive to human felicity.

The legislature also created a new county, by the name of Harford, including all that part of Baltimore county laying north and east of Little Gunpowder. Caroline county was erected out of Dorchester and Queen Anne's, the same year, and a great road directed to be made from Cumberland to the nearest boatable navigation westward of the Alleghany mountains, at the charge of the province.

At a session held in 1774, being the last under the proprietary government, further penalties were prescribed for obstructing the harbors. The principal roads to Baltimore, which in 1804, were transfered to chartered companies and turnpiked, were opened, or straightened and widened, and bills of credit loaned for making them; and a law authorising the discharge of debtors under two hundred pounds sterling, on delivery of their effects to the sheriffs, was the last which received the sanction of governor Eden. He remained undisturbed at Annapolis until June 1776, when he embarked in the British sloop of war Fowey, captain Montague, who having a flag, permitted fugitives to go on board, and caused the embarkation of Mr. Eden's baggage to be obstructed. Some British dispatches to him being intercepted by general C. Lee, the general wrote the committee at Baltimore to arrest the governor, but they referred it to the council of safety who did not think fit or necessary to comply. Joining Dunmore in the bay, the governor went to England and was knighted, but returned to Annapolis with Mr. Harford in 1784, and died near that city soon after. The members of council and of the upper-house in 1774 and the last under the proprietary, were Benedict Calvert, John Ridout, John Beale Bordley, George Stewart, Daniel of St. Thomas Jenifer, Benjamin Ogle, Philip Thomas Lee, Daniel Dulany, William Hayward, William Fitzhugh, George Plater and Edward Lee, esquires, Mr. Dulany was secratary, Mr. Fitzhugh, commissary-general, Mr. Stewart judge of the court of admiralty, and with Mr. Calvert judge of the land office, Mr. Jenifer receiver-general and agent of the proprietary. Thomas Jennings, esquire, was attorney-general and Robert Smith, esquire, surveyor-general of the *western shore*, no such officer being appointed for the other shore for some years before; Mr. Hayward was chief justice and Messrs Bordley, Jenifer, Philip T. Lee, John Leeds, John Cooke and Joseph Sim, associate judges of the provincial court.

Prepared as the people were, the distressing accounts received from Massachusetts, and the encouragement received at the same time from Virginia, the towns and counties generally assembled and elected committees to superintend the public concerns, legislative judicial and military; and, in less than one month after the close of the last assembly 1774, a convention of delegates from the towns and counties of Maryland, met at Annapolis, to concert measures for the relief of Boston, then blockaded and the redress of grievances imposed by the British government. We view with amazement, even now perhaps more than ever, the obstinacy of that infatuation with which the British ministry persisted in a system of taxation of the colonies containing at least three hundred thousand fighting men, three thousand miles off, whilst they restrained the commerce of the colonists, which alone would enable them to pay any taxes, surrounded too as that government then was, by powerful and aggravated rivals; but Providence chose to restore a natural state of independence to a part of the new world by a miraculous display of human frailty in a part of the old.

Ninety-two members attended the provincial convention, which appointed Matthew Tilghman, Thomas Johnson, Robert Goldsborough, William Paca and Samuel Chase, esquires, to represent the colony in a general congress; which they recommended to be held at Philadelphia in September following. At this congress, Georgia was not at first represented, and in which general Washington was a delegate from Virginia; a redress of grievances was sought by non-importation, to which New-York did not assent at the time, and spirited remonstrances against restrictions, taxation, &c. addressed to the people as well as to the government of England. Town and county committees were organised in pursuance of a recommendation of congress; and as occasion required, provincial conventions assembled at Annapolis. The above named gentlemen with Messrs. Bordley, Jenifer, Thomas Stone, H. Hooper, Charles Carroll of Carrollton, Edward Lloyd, James Holliday, Thomas Smith, Charles Carroll, Barrister, Richard Lloyd and Robert Alexander, were appointed a committee of correspondence; and they or some of them, with other eight or nine persons, a council of safety, from time to time, until the government under which we now live was organised. To this body great discretionary power was granted, and the *habeus corpus* was partially suspended by laws which also justly defined treasonable acts. Congress offered to contribute to the national defence, if great Britain would remove all restrictions on trade and put Americans on a footing with other subjects in this respect, in 1775, but the British government at last merely proposed the abandonment of the proceeds of the duties and to suspend the pretentions to tax America by an act of parliament.

In 1776, the Congress, in which Messrs. S. Chase, Paca, Stone and Carroll of Carrollton, represented Maryland, declared the independence of the Union; having the year before, appointed general Washington to the command of the American army stationed before Boston. Maryland received and protected the national representatives at Baltimore being threatened by the British army on the Delaware, before the end of the year.

The plan of government formed by the convention of Maryland in 1776 has received several important alterations; the counties have been divided into election districts; all white male citizens made eligable voters, and all others excluded and the manner of voting being changed fron *viva voce* to ballot. Some qualifications to offices have also been removed, but it is remarkable that all Christian *ministers* are still excluded by their profession. Eighty members, four for each county and two each for Annapolis and Baltimore form the house of delegates, being elected directly by the citizens annually, and nine senators for the western and six for the eastern-shore, elected by half the number of the delegates, every five years compose the 2d branch of the legislature. The two branches elect the governor and five councillors annually, and the governor and council appoint the judges, who hold their offices during good behaviour.

It was by the convention that Frederick county was divided into Frederick, Washington and Montgomery counties, and in 1789, Alleghany county was taken from Washington by an act of assembly, completing the present number of nineteen, eleven of which on the western and eight on the eastern side of the bay. One or two individuals at Annapolis, and as many in some of the counties, were pronounced enemies to the cause of the colonies, and underwent some persecutions and even personal violence, but the public authorities uniformly condemned such violence, and prevented any serious consequences.

"In this memorable interval between the fall of the old and the institution of the new government," says the late chancellor Hanson, in the preface to his edition of the laws, "there appeared to exist amongst us such a fund of public virtue as scarcely a parallel in the annals of the world, although many occasions occurred in which intemperate zeal transported men beyond the just bounds of moderation, not a single person fell a victim to the oppression of this irregular government;" and he continues, "without this virtue, the opposition of a country unskilled in war, destitute of arms, inferior far in numbers, and wanting almost every thing for which it had before relied solely on its now inveterate enemies, the opposition of such a people to the efforts of the most powerful nation on the globe would have been feeble indeed."

Besides their own entire self-government immediately obtained, the citizens would have enjoyed a free intercourse with all the world but for the war. The church establishment was abolished, however, all sects of christians being equally privileged and protected, and taxes were to be no longer levied on the individuals per *poll*, or by classes and numbers, but according to their property, and as far as practicable, their means of enjoyment.

The constitution was carried into effect with great unanimity early in 1777. After the new senate and delegates had elected Thomas Johnson, esquire, governor, and Messrs. Josiah Polk, John Rogers, Edward Lloyd, Thomas Sim Lee and Joseph Sim, councillors, Messrs Carroll and Brice declining, they proceeded to provide for the exigencies of a state of war.* The continental and state money was made a legal tender, and the currency which had been sometime uncertain, was fixed at the rate of seven shillings and six pence to the dollar.

The recruiting service was promoted, and the state sent to the army, under general Smallwood and others at different times, about fourteen thousand regular troops, besides drafts of militia;

* Governor Johnson being twice re-elected and having served the three political years limited by the constitution, was succeeded by the following gentlemen at the several periods annexed to their names respectively:

Thomas Sim Lee,	1779	John Francis Mercer,	1801
William Paca,	1782	Robert Bowie,	1803
William Smallwood,	1785	Robert Wright,	1806
John Eager Howard,	1788	Edward Lloyd,	1809
George Plater,	1791	Robert Bowie,	1811
Thomas Sim Lee,	179[illegible]	Levin Winder,	1812
John Hoskins Stone,	1794	Charles Ridgely, of Hampton,	1815
John Henry,	1797	Charles Goldsborough,	1818
Benjamin Ogle,	1798	Samuel Sprigg,	1819

and a flotilla of gallies and small vessels were provided. Among other gentlemen who entered the continental army from this state were Messrs. Uriah Forrest and Benjamin Ford, of St. Mary's county, James Wilkinson of Calvert, Philip Steuart and John H. Stone of Charles, Mordecai Gist, Samuel Smith, John E. Howard and Nicholas Rogers of Baltimore, Josias Carvel Hall of Harford, Nathaniel Ramsay of Cecil, Otho H. Williams of Washington, William Richardson and Peter Adams of Caroline, James Hindman of Talbot, John Gunby and Levin Winder of Somerset, Moses Rawlings and Patrick Sim of Anne Arundel, Edward Tillard, Thomas Woolford and Ludwick Weltner of Frederick.

The trade of the Chesapeake was interrupted very early, and in the course of the year, Lord Howe landed the British army under his brother, sir William, on Elk-neck; from whence they proceeded to Philadelphia, after their success at Brandywine. In the same year also, the British army under Burgoyne capitulated at Saratogo to general Gates. Charles Carroll, barrister, Solomon Wright and John Beale Bordley, esquires, were appointed judges of the general court, and Thomas Jennings, esquire, attorney-general. Thomas Harwood, junior, esquire, was made treasurer of the western-shore, and William Hindman, esquire, treasurer of the eastern-shore.

In 1778, the alliance was made with France, and the articles of confederation published by congress, and in 1781 count de Grasse entered the bay; and with the allied troops, general Washington, captured the British army and lord Cornwallis at York. The same year, Maryland having vainly waited for assurances that the western country would be considered the joint territory of the confederacy, assented to the articles of confederation. Provision being made for a court of appeals, Benjamin Rumsey, Benjamin Mackall, the fourth, Thomas Jones, Solomon Wright, and James Murray, esquires, were appointed judges.

In 1780, the quit rents were abolished as *an acknowledgement of a seigniory incompatible with the* [illegible] *sovereignty of this free and independent state,* of which other colonists were freed already, as it was said; and every landed estate became allodial instead of feudal, but the equal inheritance of all children of intestates was not determined against the *heir at law,* until six years after. In the meantime, all British property was confiscated; the proprietary's manors and reserved lands fell to the state of course, and a treble tax was imposed on *non-jurors* to redeem the black and red money, by which the other was drawn out of circulation at various rates of depreciation and in succession.

There was however a surplus received, the interest of which, added to the receipts from duties before the federal constitution was adopted, licences and fines, defrayed the public expenditures of the state, and general assessments of supplies ceased in 1785; that is, before the monies borrowed of Messrs Vanstaphorst, of Amsterdam, had been repaid; being, we believe, half a million, for the loan was payable in tobacco, and cost by the rise of that article after the peace, as much or more in damages as was first borrowed; or the recovery of the British bank stock, which amounted to six hundred and fifty thousand dollars.†

The claims which Mr. Harford came to urge in person after the war, amounting, for the quit rents at twenty-five years purchase, to six hundred and ninety-one thousand, nine hundred

† In 1816 exports of domestic produce from the state of Maryland according to the official returns published,

amounted to - - -	$4,834,490
and foreign products to - -	2,504,277
making together - , -	7,338,767

The registered tonnage of vessels employed in foreign trade

was - - - - - -	83,123 tons.
enrolled in the coasting trade -	64,161
licenced vessels in the same trade	8,777
making together	156,061 tons.

and the revenue on customs received by the United States from the State of Maryland, exclusive of drawbacks and expences of collection, amonted to 2,771,910 dollars.

In 1798, George Town, with about fifty square miles, having been ceeded to the United States in 1791, there were assessed in Maryland, five million, four hundred and forty-

and sixty-five dollars, and sixty-seven cents; and for lands, to eight hundred and seventy-three thousand, one hundred and seventy-six dolls. were rejected, but he has received with other loyalists a considerable indemnity from the British government as did Mrs. Browning and Mrs. Eden, a lesser sum between them, and about the sum of ten thousand pounds sterling was also obtained by Mr. Harford out of the state's stock then in England.

Having by the peace of 1783 secured their own independence, congress setting at Annapolis, received the resignation of general Washington, and our legislature immediately prohibited the introduction of slaves altogether, and declared the persons and property of free blacks within the guardianship of the laws of the state, and soon after abolished the claims of the eldest

four thousand, two hundred and seventy-two acres of land, amount - - - - - 21,634,004 dollars
16,932 houses amount to - 10,738,286

32,372,290 dollars:

and in 1814, the lands and improvements, were valued at - - - 106,490,638 dollars
and the slaves at - - - 16,086,934

122,577,572 dollars.

Upon which there were received in 1816, $149,099
And by other internal taxes, - - 349,847
The state's capital stock, as stated to the legislature in 1820, of which there was in the U. States'

stock six per cent. - - -	$133,717 83
United States' three per cent. -	335,104 74
Stock in the Potowmack Company	120,444 44
Loan to Do.	30,000 00
Stock in different banks of the state	516,100 00
Do. Frederick & York Turnpike Co.	15,000 00
Do. Union Manufacturing Company	10,000 00
Debts due by individuals, loans to schools, &c. - -	67,766 12
amounted to	$1,223,133 13‡

‡ *This sum is stated according to the* votes *and* proceedings, *though apparently short five thousand dollars.*

sons and divided estates equally among children of intestates, extended the privileges and income of the colleges at Annapolis and Chester united for a university, which they held until 1805. Lands in Alleghany county were given the soldiers and the land office was again opened for the sale of the vacancies at from two shillings to ten shillings per acre. Companies were incorporated to open and improve the navigation of the Patowmack and Susquehanna rivers; the jurisdiction of the former, the bay and Pocomoke rivers being adjusted on equal and just

The capital was stated in 1801, to amount to one million, one hundred and thirty-six thousand. If the three per cents. were sold at the rate now current, it would appear that there has been little increase or diminution of capital since that time.

From the statement of the last and present years it appears that the annual expences of about one hundred and eighty

pensioners, are - - - -	18,000 dollars
Donations to colleges - - -	12,000
Penitentiary charges - - -	10,000
Legislature one session - -	35,000
Judges salaries - - - -	32,400
Governor, Chancellor, & other officers	12,600
Total	120,000 dollars.

That the interest from U.States' stock is	18,000
Fines and licences, retailers, pedlars, marriages, &c. - - -	35,000
Dividands of banks and roads -	26,000
Sales of land, interest on debts, &c.	21,000
Total	100,000 dollars.
Leaving an annual deficit of about	20,000 dollars.

and the sum of six hundred and fifty thousand dolls. received for the states' stock in England in 1805, principally advanced on account of the United States in the late war, but returned for the most part, is absorbed. At the same time the half pay of the revolutionary soldiers has been increased in number of pensioners and the dividends on bank stock has fallen.; still the only material consideration is, whether the investments have been made in such institutions as are best calculated to advance the interest of the state by the advancement of the peoples means of prosperity and happiness.

terms with Virginia, by Messrs. Jenifer, Stone and S. Chase, on the part of Maryland.

Loans had been obtained abroad by the State, as mentioned before, and by the United States, during the war; and with the latter, Mr. Robert Morris was enabled to establish a Bank, and provide for the most urgent expenses, after the fall of the paper money. A continental debt of about sixty millions, required at that time, great exertions even to pay the interest, and while the importations from England were excessive, the citizens were excluded from some of her dominions, and had not shipping to be the carriers of all their own saleable products any where.

Some of the States again resorted to paper money, but Maryland, by the perseverance of the smallest branch of the Legislature, refrained from a system which had been so injurious to many. Though in 1776 and 1777, indispensible, it was otherwise now, in a state of peace and independence. The money created must have been loaned out at some risk, or lavished in expenses, and a people who are debtors or creditors of their government, are not the most likely to maintain its principles. So also, they who pay no taxes, or think they have nothing to pay, are too apt to suffer all other matters of government, to become a sport or jest, and be in danger of losing their best privileges by their indifference. By the federal constitution, the power of emitting bills of credit was taken away from the State governments, but they may still raise money by loans or taxes; and any government is limited in other respects, to little purpose perhaps, which can borrow money or lay contributions for all sums, by all modes, and give and take bounties at its own discretion. For as to debts contracted by loans or otherwise, too many do not think of the contracts until they must be paid, and few prefer future to present advantage; with a little art, old debts are paid by new loans, until the amount has accumulated to such a degree that it is esteemed madness to talk of redemption; and, as to taxes, there is a paradox of which governments that are popular especially, will be tempted to avail themselves; they will lay the contribution upon articles which pass through many hands between the maker and the consumer, by which the tax has as many advocates as contributors; each one retains not only that portion which was first *bonded for*, but a premium for himself; vainly will they tax luxuries; they that buy or consume them, are they who fix the price of labour, because the means are universal, and the people may be ground down to poverty almost without knowing the art or the artist; and here is the paradox, that which is least burthensome is the most offensive, whilst that which extracts the most from the hands of labour is least opposed.

Maryland and some other States laid taxes and duties for the payment of continental debts and the support of the confederation. A tender made of power to levy a duty of five per cent. on all imports, and offers to agree to a general act of navigation by this State, were not accepted by Congress for want of the assent of others, and a deficiency was constantly experienced.

This, with the individual embarrassments of the people, produced the convention which first met at Annapolis in 1786, and in Philadelphia in 1787, when the present Constitution of the United States was formed; Maryland being represented by Daniel of St. Thomas Jenifer, James McHenry, Danl. Carroll, of Dudington, and Luther Martin, Esquires.

The Constitution by them proposed, was adopted very soon, and almost unanimously by the people of this State, and went into operation in 1789 under the presidency of Gen. Washington.

The form of this government is not unlike that of Maryland and other State governments. Its powers are expressly limited, "to provide for the common defence and general welfare of the United States," by enumerated grants, which include the regulation of foreign intercourse, commerce and navigation, making war or peace, treaties of alliance or commerce, establishing and maintaining armies and navies, naturalization and bankrupt laws, coining money, transportation of letters, granting patents, courts of justice, systems of revenue, &c. Each State is represented by two senators, and representatives of the people according to their numbers; Maryland having at this time nine, and chooses eleven electors of President and Vice-President, all at different intervals of time. It is an efficient if not energetic form of government, and has been a basis for new modeling several State governments, though it can never, like they sometimes had, become by *fair means*, a depositary of the whole sovereignty of the people.

In the life of Washington, as written by Judge Marshall, may be seen the history of the opposition to the internal taxes laid by Congress; for which Maryland sent troops to the westward; and to the neutral attitude assumed by the government in 1793.

Thence arose the division of the citizens into two political parties, which was confirmed by the Treaty of Amity with England in 1794, and the hostilities against the French in 1798.

In other books or treatises will be seen the extraordinary increase of our wealth and population, notwithstanding the obstructions to which this nation was exposed since the close of the last century, by the continued revolutions in Europe, and the wars which they caused; difficulties which continued under the successors of Washington, until in 1807, all foreign trade was suspended above a year, by acts of Congress, and in 1812, the United States were forced from their wonted neutrality, and plunged into another war with Great Britain.

The effects of this war upon the State of Maryland, are too recent to be forgotten. The British landed on Patuxent in 1814, and captured the seat of the general government, but failed in an attempt upon Baltimore soon after.

Though the treaty which restored peace to us, was silent on the major as well as the minor objects of the war, and though we had incurred a debt as much greater than that of the former war, as the means of the country were then less than at the present period, the United States were relieved by the general cessation of hostilities, from the practical evils of disputed principles assumed by the belligerents in relation to neutrals; and, early reverses having changed the scene of action more favourably to our arms on land, the close of it was accompanied by achievements there, equal to those which had been effected at sea, and a confidence in the national prowess arose becoming a people arrived at maturity.

A CRONOLOGICAL LIST

OF THE

SOVEREIGNS OF ENGLAND, THE PROPRIETARIES, AND GOVERNORS,

During the Proprietary Government of Maryland.

YEAR.	SOVEREIGNS OF ENGLAND.	PROPRIETARIES OF MARYLAND.	GOVERNORS OF MARYLAND.
1632	Charles the first.	Cecilius Calvert, 2d Lord Baltimore.	
1633			Leonard Calvert.
1643			Giles Brent, deputy.
1644			Leonard Calvert.
1647			Thomas Green, deputy.
1648			William Stone.
1649	Parliament.		
1654	Oliver Cromwell, protector.		William Fuller and others, commissioners.
1656			Josias Fendall.
1658	Richard Cromwell, protector.		
1660	Charles the second.		Philip Calvert.
1661			Charles Calvert.
1669			Philip Calvert and others, deputies.
1671			Charles Calvert.
1675			Thomas Notley.
1676		Charles Calvert, 3d Lord Baltimore.	The Proprietary—Cecilius Calvert, Jesse Wharton and others, deputies.
1677			Thomas Notley.
1680			The Proprietary.
1684			B. L. Calvert, G. Talbot & others, deputies.

[illegible]			William Joseph, president.
1688	William and Mary.		
1689			Convention, K. Cheseldine and others.
1691			Lionel Copley.
1693			Edmond Andross.
1694			Francis Nicholson.
1695	William the third.		
1698			Nathaniel Blakiston.
1702	Anne.		
1703			Thomas Tench, president.
1704			John Seymour.
1709			Edward Lloyd, president.
1714	George the first.		John Hart.
1715		Benedict L. Calvert, 4th Ld Baltimore Charles Calvert, 5th Lord Baltimore.	
1720	George the second.		Charles Calvert.
1727			Benedict L. Calvert.
1731			Samuel Ogle.
1732			The Proprietary.
1733			Samuel Ogle.
1742			Thomas Bladen.
1746			Samuel Ogle.
1751		Frederick Calvert, 6th Lord Baltimore.	
1752			Benjamin Tasker, president.
1753			Horatio Sharpe.
1760	George the third.		
1768			Robert Eden
1771		Henry Harford, Esq.	
1776	Convention.	Convention.	Convention.

ERRATA FOR THE SKETCHES.

Page.	*Line.*	*For.* — *Read.*
1	2	Cecelius—Cecilius
5	29	chattles—chattels
9	37	fugatives—fugitives
10	12	1738—1638
11	24	Patomack—Patowmack
	33	1346—1646
14	1	were—was
	31	to—of
17	2	Nicholls—Sedgewicke
19	36	this—Fendall's
22	18	1763—1663
	21	1759—1769
	24	1664—1663
24	9	had—has
25	4	1761—1671
28	6	revolution the—revolution was 44 years, the
35	17	the other half—half the Tobacco duty
37	23	Capitol—Capital
		Protestant—Royal
39	12	Blakston—Blakiston
41	35 36	were—was
44	3	again—still
46	16	were—was
58	9	1674—1764
60	28	Piney—Pinkney
62	26	least eighth—least an eighth
74	22	Duddington—Rock Creek

www.ingramcontent.com/pod-product-compliance
Lightning Source LLC
LaVergne TN
LVHW020655100826
845148LV00012B/2500

* 9 7 8 0 7 8 8 4 4 8 1 4 0 *